ENLIGHTENED SPIRITUALITY

Past Light on Present Life: Theology, Ethics, and Spirituality

Roger Haight, SJ, Alfred Pach III,
and *Amanda Avila Kaminski,* series editors

These volumes are offered to the academic community of teachers and learners in the fields of Christian history, theology, ethics, and spirituality. They introduce classic texts by authors whose contributions have markedly affected the development of Christianity, especially in the West. The texts are accompanied by an introductory essay on context and key themes and followed by an interpretation that dialogically engages the original message with the issues of ethics, theology, and spirituality in the present.

Enlightened Spirituality

IMMANUEL KANT, PAUL TILLICH,
AND REINHOLD NIEBUHR

EDITED AND WITH COMMENTARY BY
Roger Haight, SJ, Alfred Pach III,
and Amanda Avila Kaminski

FORDHAM UNIVERSITY PRESS   NEW YORK 2024

This series has been generously supported by a theological education grant from the E. Rhodes and Leona B. Carpenter Foundation.

Immanuel Kant, "Preface," "First Section—Transition from the Common Rational Knowledge of Morality to the Philosophical," and selection from "Second Section—Transition from Popular Moral Philosophy to the Metaphysic of Morals," are reprinted from *Fundamental Principles of the Metaphysic of Morals* (trans. Thomas Kingsbill Abbott; Urbana, Illinois: Project Gutenberg). Public domain.

Selection from Paul Tillich, *Morality and Beyond* is reprinted with the permission of Theodore N. Farris, as copyright owner and proprietor of the literary rights of Paul Tillich. Originally published by Harper & Row (1963).

"The Relevance of the Christian View of Man" is reprinted from Reinhold Niebuhr, *The Nature and Destiny of Man: A Christian Interpretation.* (Louisville: Westminster John Knox Press, 2021), 123–36. Used with permission.

Fordham University Press has no responsibility for the persistence or accuracy of URLs for external or third-party Internet websites referred to in this publication and does not guarantee that any content on such websites is, or will remain, accurate or appropriate.

Fordham University Press also publishes its books in a variety of electronic formats. Some content that appears in print may not be available in electronic books.

Visit us online at www.fordhampress.com.

Library of Congress Cataloging-in-Publication Data available online at https://catalog.loc.gov.

Printed in the United States of America

26 25 24   5 4 3 2 1

First edition

Contents

ENLIGHTENED SPIRITUALITY

I

Introduction to the Authors and the Texts

Immanuel Kant towers above the horizon of Western philosophy. He marks a before and an after that reach to the present time: In one way or another we are all neo- or post-Kantians. Just as Thomas Aquinas proposed a deep structure for spirituality, so too Kant represents a different interpretation of the foundations of the metaphysics of being a Christian. As Aquinas has to be situated in the thirteenth century, where he profited by the new wave of Aristotelian thinking in Europe, so too must Kant be seen as representing a turn to the subject in philosophy and to the critical questioning of the Enlightenment.

Kant was born in 1724 in Koenigsberg in northern Germany into a Lutheran Pietist family that was attached to a local church. As a child, he attended for eight years the Pietist school run by the pastor of the church and learned Latin. He then studied theology at the University of Koenigsberg. But his interests gradually shifted to mathematics, science, and philosophy. He was attracted to the work of Isaac Newton's (1643–1727) physics. He remained a Christian but distanced himself from formal doctrinal teaching. For years before becoming a university professor, Kant worked as a family tutor.

As a philosopher, Kant stands by himself but in conversation with many. He worked in the tradition of Descartes (1596–1650), who, in the wake of the Reformation, asked the question of the grounds of certain knowledge and found the answer in the knowing subject. Philosophy turned a corner from arguing on the basis of observed causality. Because Kant was deeply influenced by Newton's synthesis of empirical knowledge of the world, when David Hume (1711–76) affirmed that we can really know nothing more than what sense data reveal to us, Kant took notice. Roger Scruton describes Kant's project as mediating between a rationalism that thinks it can transcend opinion to reach certitude and Hume's empiricism that reduces knowledge to the subjectivity of perception.[1]

Kant became an archetypal Enlightenment figure, and much will have to be said about that. The many thinkers who made up the movement frequently bear the title "*illuminati*," the enlightened. This immediately surrounds the title of this volume as somewhat ironic because proud high-mindedness does not typify Christian spirituality. But we may allow it when enlightenment means "questioning" or "critical" or simply seeing things in a new light of reason without necessarily being reductionist. Such a stance finds far more resonance today than it did in the churches of the eighteenth century. Kant was addressing questions that everyone asks today. Can we really overcome self- or group-interest to know what is objectively good? Is there any truly objective value and universal norm for human behavior? If "spirituality" refers to the way persons and groups live their lives, they have to have some answer to those questions, and, in our culture, spirituality has to address the test of critical reason.

This Introduction focuses on Kant's text *Fundamental Principles of the Metaphysic of Morals*. It turns first to the Enlightenment to situate the author and text and to show the uncanny familiarity and distance of its position. It then introduces the author but passes quickly to an outline of his argument. This first part of this volume then introduces the essays of Paul Tillich and Reinhold Niebuhr. These great twentieth-century American thinkers take up the conversation with Kant relative to the bearing of his views on present-day self-understanding and spirituality.

Enlightenment

Two essential factors help to locate the thought of Immanuel Kant: his critical philosophy and his representation of the Enlightenment. In philosophy he exemplifies the turn to the human subject as focus of attention. With Descartes, philosophy shifted from reasoning about the objective world in front of us and perceived by common sense, to a critical examination of the human knower, the subject. Philosophy about the world is channeled through epistemology, or reflection on the process of human knowing. Objective reasoning about the world as it appears before us does not produce agreement. Critical philosophy of the subject by contrast supposes that human beings possess a universal or common or transcendental human subjectivity based on the unity of the species.[2] By penetrating the stages and rules of perception and reasoning, one can attain a common philosophy of knowledge itself and through it a communicable if not common appreciation of reality. These themes of critical philosophy are perfectly exemplified in this work of Kant on ethics. He finds the universal norm for assessing goodness within the human subject.

One also has to allude to the Enlightenment as a context for Kant's thinking. In one sense, the Enlightenment refers to a group of thinkers, mainly philosophers, who wrote between the time of the death of Descartes to the end of the eighteenth century. The movement is often dated more narrowly as the one hundred years between the English and French revolutions, 1689 and 1789. Some of the people involved were Locke, Newton, Voltaire, Franklin, Hume, Rousseau, Diderot, Lessing, Jefferson, and Kant. These were the *illuminati*, who proposed to offer light to people whose eyes were closed, who needed to be awakened from their dogmatic slumber.[3]

But the Enlightenment was more than a group of philosophers. Over the years they created a cultural climate or milieu that became an ideological construct.[4] It consists of a mix of rationalism, the conviction that reason alone could broker universal truth, and a recognition of the new body of knowledge that was being assembled in the world of science. The sciences had turned to close empirical observation and measurement and gathered an enormous amount of empirical data. It is hard for people today to appreciate the accomplishment of Newton's synthesis of the collected empirical information of his day into a unity of principles and mathematical methods. And they worked.

A number of keywords may be used as a shorthand way of characterizing this intellectual culture. The listing provides no more than a notional or abstract framework of impressions. But the text of Kant will come alive as it illustrates this new confidence in critical reason. It reaches the height that Aquinas himself displayed in answering so many questions on the basis of Aristotelian reason in the context of Christian faith.

Science. The rise of the sciences of course helps explain the genesis of the Enlightenment. Brief reflection on the shift of our species's self-understanding that Copernicus, Kepler, and Galileo mediated will help appreciation of what is going on intellectually during this period.

Reason. Many felt that human beings were coming of age; they should use their reason and dare to think.[5]

Criticism. Critical questioning (criticism or critique) lies at the heart of this culture. This defines what intelligence or reason can and should do because of what they essentially are. The way to learn consists of reflecting, calling into question, doubting, and reformulating. The process suggests negativity, but the activity reflects inquiry, seeing more broadly and considering more deeply. Criticism translates the virtue of wonder into seeking further rather than taking for granted.[6]

The Greeks. Enlightenment thinkers loved and appealed to the classic rationalism of the Greeks. Socrates was a cultural hero who represented criticism, self-knowledge, self-mastery and balance in ethics.

Authority. The antithesis of reason and criticism consisted of authority, tradition, and ultimately authoritarianism. These obstacles to discovery were lodged mainly in the churches and their allies in government. The Enlightenment stood for an attack on religion and especially on the church; it was anti-clerical because every new discovery seemed to be contested by religious traditions.

Disenchantment. The critique of religion went deeper; religion began to mean superstition as the world ceased to be a place of God's disclosure. "The disenchanted universe of the Enlightenment is a natural universe."[7]

Freedom. On every front "freedom" was the slogan of the Enlightenment: political, social, religious, individual, economic. It did not of course just fall into place, but the ideal was proposed and attracted commitment.

Autonomy. Law and order imposed from the outside is dehumanizing and oppressive: heteronomous. Order in the various spheres of life comes from below, through human reason and freedom itself. Kant's *Metaphysic of Morals* is this sentiment's perfect Enlightenment argument.

Peter Gay used these broad strokes to draw out in detail the inner logic running through three generations of thinkers. One should note that these themes are not intrinsically hostile to spirituality or even to religion, unless one reduces the latter to their objective institutional frameworks. This can be shown by recognizing the degree to which many of these convictions allowed spirituality to thrive in the United States, which was built on Enlightenment foundations.

Kant's Metaphysic of Morals

In his metaphysics of knowing, Kant tried to reconcile rationalism and the empiricism of the scientist or the ultimate
skeptic regarding speculative thought. Through critical reflection he showed a middle way between conceptualism and raw
perception. "Without sensibility no object would be given to
us, without understanding no object would be thought.
Thoughts without content are empty; intuitions without
concepts are blind."[8] Analogously, in order to find a universal
norm for moral behavior, he argues from moral experience
itself to its *a priori* or universal structure. He appeals to moral
sensibility itself rather than try to prove that it exists. Although
the work seems laborious, it appeals to experience, and one
can readily follow its steps. The following propositions para-
phrase the development of the argument.

The purpose of the metaphysics of morals is to ground the
idea of duty and moral law in pure reason and thus show its
universality. This defines what Kant means by the metaphysical foundations of morality, its being rooted in reason, and
the necessary logic of pure reason. Because rationality is a
given and is universal, structured by the necessity of logical
thought itself, morality finds its foundation there, one that
bears an absolute character. Kant's move seeks to free morality
from culture, society, history, emotion, feeling, and authority:
All of these things are variable and serve only to muddy moral
waters. By contrast, the universal ground for ethics lies in
rationality itself, *a priori*, before all experience, in the very
structure of practical human reason.

*The basis of morality is a good will; only a good will is a
good in itself.* This principle is meant to establish the premise
that morality emerges not from outside the human subject
but from within. "Morality" refers to a quality of human action.
The human subject has within itself the grounds of ethics.
The basis of morality lies within the will or is the will itself.
What this means can be read in what it negates. Morality does

not originate outside the will; it is not imposed by an external law or authority; it does not lie in the end, or the consequence, or the object of an action. The ground of morality is contained within the autonomy of the will itself, a conviction that illustrates pure Enlightenment reasoning.

A good will is one that responds from a sense of duty and law. The term "duty" suddenly appears in Kant's text as if everyone is familiar with it. An experience of duty forms the basis of Kant's ethics. He defines "duty" in this way: *"Duty is the necessity of acting from respect for the law."*[9] The idea is to ensure the internal, *a priori* character of willing as the determining factor of morality. He consistently contrasts duty to the "end" as that which makes the good will good, presumably as in teleological ethics.[10] In contrast to this, Kant says that an action has moral worth only when it is done from duty, when an internal sense of duty alone motivates it. He considered acting from duty as an autonomous act, a pure act of the will, as distinct from external motivating factors. For example, a particular goal that one aims at would be an external criterion defining the action as moral; judging morality by consequences also entails an external criterion. Duty reflects an inward respect for an inner law, not an inclination from or toward something outside the human person.

The will contains a categorical imperative to act according to the universal law of reason. Kant then goes on to analyze the categorical imperative entailed in the experience of duty. He frequently calls it *the* categorical imperative to show that foundationally there is only one. But the one imperative has a variety of different forms or formulations that bring out its different aspects and fill out Kant's moral theory. The basic logic appears in the following generalized formula: One should act in any particular case or situation in such a way that my subjective principle of willing, my maxim, may be considered a universal law. A "maxim" refers to both a principle and a subjective motivating factor.[11] In other words, I should so act that I would want all other human beings to act in the same

way. I should be able to universalize my subjective will and
be able consistently to conceive it as universally applicable.
In Kant's words, this categorical imperative says, "I am never
to act otherwise than so *that I could also will that my maxim
should become a universal law.*"[12]

This categorical imperative, as opposed to a hypothetical
or conditional imperative, is the universal, formal, and autonomous metaphysical foundation of morality in pure reason.
Both ideas, "categorical" and "imperative," deserve comment.
An imperative is a command; in this case it is a formulated
command of reason. Duty and the imperative it relays to
consciousness ground the obligation stemming from the objective law of reason. To call it categorical means that it is
absolute and not relative to anything else. It arises out of the
autonomy of the will and human reason; morality does not
finally depend on any external circumstances or the end or
the consequences of an action. It arises out of the will itself
rather than from outside human self-consciousness. For example, ethics and morality cannot consist in imitating the
behavior of an outside example. And he illustrates this with
the dramatic example of Christ: Morality is not imitation of
Christ. Or, to be more precise, the external imitation of Christ
is not what makes an action moral.

Kant contrasts the categorical imperative with a hypothetical imperative. The "hypothesis" makes the imperative conditional: If one wants to be in Southeast Asia and is not there,
one has to travel. The doing of something is imperative, but
only on the supposition or the condition of another premise
external to the action itself. This is how Kant views other
definitions of the good; they depend on an end, or a goal, or
the character of the objective consequences of an action. If
you want to be happy, or fulfilled, then you must do this. By
contrast, the foundation for morality in Kant's system is pure
reason itself. The imperative for action arises out of reason
itself independently of ends, consequences, or any outside
factor or condition or circumstance.

The one general formula of the categorical imperative has three other specified conceptions. There is one categorical imperative, but it can be formulated in three different ways to bring out different aspects of this formal ethics. The first formula, scarcely different from the generic categorical imperative, states that to be moral, one must be able to universalize one's maxim. It stresses the universality and unity of all morality. The second formula states that one should never treat another human being merely as a means. Human beings are ends in themselves. Kant establishes this principle on the basis that every person declaring it in his or her own regard makes it universal.[13] This formulation serves as a criterion for measuring absolute ends, human beings, and relative ends or means.

The third formula or practical principle of the categorical imperative says that every willing human subject is not only an obedient will but also a legislating will. It stresses the autonomy of human reason and will; law emerges out of the human subject. Kant also speaks here about the kingdom of ends. This is a utopian society in which all human beings treat others not as means but as ends, and all the ends exist in harmony. This is the ideal social result of Kant's ethics and the practical goal it envisages. But it is not an outside goal; it emerges from within the human subject. In this respect, the kingdom or rule of God is a religious symbol for the kingdom of ends in Kant's thought.

Conclusion. Kant's enlightenment ethics finds its source within the human subject and a universal experience of duty, an imperative to respect the inward law of human reason itself. This law has a general formula, but various formulas bring out different aspects. The first stresses its universality; the second stresses the absolute character of the human being as an end and never merely a means; the third projects the law of reason into a social condition of harmony where all would treat others as ends and not merely means.

Scruton sums up the achievement of Kant's philosophy of morals around the notion of human "autonomy." Kant explains the distinction between a person and a thing; his ethics rests on personalism. He explains the absolute character of morality. He locates morality within each person as deliberate intentionality and distinguishes it from inclination or emotion without excluding those dimensions of personal experience. His argument emerges out of the inner conviction that all people are created equal as subjects. The autonomy of the rational person becomes the basis of his moral system.[14] He distinguishes morality from acting according to the law as command from outside the self. Duty comes from within and is the vehicle for discovering the universal good.[15]

Paul Tillich

The turn to Paul Tillich and Reinhold Niebuhr helps create a bridge between the philosophical culture of the Enlightenment and the present time. The two essays open up a current theological horizon for appreciating Kant's lesson for Christian spirituality. Tillich was born in 1886 in Germany, where his father was a minister in the Lutheran tradition. He studied in Berlin and did theological studies at the University of Halle from 1905 to 1912, where, under Martin Kähler, he closely studied the religious philosopher Friedrich Schelling. He was ordained and served as a military chaplain during World War I. After the war he taught at several universities and wrote extensively from an engaged religious-socialist perspective. Forbidden to teach in Germany by the Nazi regime in 1933, he moved that same year to Union Theological Seminary in New York, where he taught for twenty-two years. He taught subsequently at Harvard and at the University of Chicago before he died in 1965. His major work was his *Systematic Theology* in three volumes (1951–63); many other writings reached a wider public. He was one of the three most important systematic theologians of the twentieth century.

Tillich was an existential theologian who turned to an analysis of the human subject as the place where the meaning of religious faith and beliefs can be discussed. The bearing of scripture and traditional teachings has to be shown to correlate with the deep experiences of life in order for them to make sense and be the guides to life they claim to be. This appeal to the experience of human existence itself marks an existential theologian and immediately relates reflection to personal spirituality, the way one leads one's life.

In "The Religious Dimension of the Moral Imperative," Tillich comments on Kant's ethical system and relates it to religion and thus implicitly to spirituality.[16] He makes three essential points that begin to illuminate its significance for spirituality. First of all, Tillich confirms Kant's view that morality, as manifested in an unconditional imperative, emerges from *within* human existence. Morality does not consist of a heteronomous relationship to God. Law emerges not from an external source but from the reflective self-transcendence of freedom itself that defines human existence as person and as responsible.

Tillich then points out that the intrinsic link between morality and religion does not consist in a set of commandments: "[T]he religious dimension of the moral imperative is its unconditional character."[17] The connection with religious faith does not refer to the content but to the form in which the imperative of moral decision is cast: its formal character of "ought" and its moral seriousness. Tillich defines religious faith formally as being ultimately concerned or engaged. The religious character of morality lies in the ultimacy or unconditional quality of the inner demand: "[T]here is a religious dimension in the moral imperative itself."[18]

Finally, Tillich shows that ethics does not come from religion; rather, religion comes from ethics. The notion that ethics comes from religion undercuts the very idea of secular ethics. If the categorical imperative were attached to specific commands of God, it would deprive everyday temporal life of an ethical depth. Tillich therefore echoes Kant's insistence that the moral imperative does not consist of a specific objective content called the will of God. Rather than an external will imposed upon humanity by an external legislator, the will of God becomes an intrinsic part of human existence itself. "For us the 'Will of God' is manifest in our essential being; and only because of this can we accept the moral imperative as valid."[19] In sum, the ethical sense is universal, and it manifests the ultimate seriousness of human existence itself. In this sense one can also say that secular ethics has a religious dimension that is manifest in the absoluteness of categorical imperative.

As a postscript, Tillich comments on the idea of "conscience" relative to the categorical imperative. He wants to dissociate "conscience" from objective commands and relate it to the formal character of the categorical imperative. "Conscience is the consciousness of the 'categorical imperative,' but it is not the consciousness of a special content of this imperative. 'Conscience is a consciousness which itself is a duty.' It is a duty to have a conscience, to be conscientious."[20]

Reinhold Niebuhr

Reinhold Niebuhr was born in Missouri in 1892, the son of a minister of a Lutheran and Reformed church who had immigrated to the United States. Reinhold went to evangelical schools—Elmhurst College and Eden Theological Seminary—before finishing his theological education at Yale University with a bachelor of divinity degree and then an MA in 1915, the same year he was ordained in the Evangelical Synod. Niebuhr then pastored an evangelical church in Detroit, where he was outspoken on social issues and wrote as a critic of capitalism and as an advocate for Christian socialism. In 1928 he joined the faculty of Union Theological Seminary in New

York; he helped to bring Paul Tillich to Union and taught there until his retirement in 1960.

Niebuhr had an outsized influence on American political and social life. His "critical realism" recognizes the gap between the rule of God and actual history and modifies spiritual expectations for society. The rule of God and Christian ethics are always a work in progress. The rule of God always stands judgment on human efforts and actual historical arrangements.[21] His best-known work is *The Nature and Destiny of Man, I–II* (1941–43), in which he reworked his Gifford Lectures. As teacher, preacher, writer, and indefatigable speaker, he left his mark on Christian theology especially through his critical realist social ethic.

In the brief excerpt from *The Nature and Destiny of Man* offered here, Niebuhr associates himself with a common view that conscience provides the "place," if not the faculty, for an encounter with God.[22] For Niebuhr, one develops a religious sense through conscience, and this becomes a vehicle for general revelation. Two notions command attention here: what he means by general revelation and the role of conscience or a moral sense within it.

First, Niebuhr distinguishes between general revelation and special or particular revelation to a group in history. They depend on each other. Without public historical revelation, private revelation would be diffuse and without precise content. "Private revelation is, in a sense, synonymous with 'general' revelation ... the consciousness of every person that his life touches a reality beyond himself, a reality deeper and higher than the system of nature in which he stands."[23] All people have the possibility for this experience; it is not direct or expressly formulated as revelation, but implied in all human experience. "The soul which reaches the uttermost rims of its own consciousness must also come in contact with God, for God impinges upon that consciousness."[24]

Niebuhr says that this general revealing of God to the human person has two characteristics. He accepts the analysis of Friedrich Schleiermacher in part: We become conscious of God in an experience of "unqualified dependence." But there is more to it than that. "An equally important characteristic of the experience of God is the sense of being seen, commanded, judged and known from beyond ourselves," and this experience "is in some sense identical [to] or associated with what is usually called 'conscience.'"[25] The result is that God is revealed generally to all human beings through conscience, or, at least, conscience is part of a common possibility of a religious experience.

But at this point Niebuhr breaks out of Kant's enlightened mindset. Relying on the idea of conscience, Niebuhr thinks of consciousness of God as entailing a sense that includes God's negative judgment on human sin. Human beings stand in relation to God as both the transcendent source of being and as the arbiter of right and wrong and moral innocence and guilt. This second dimension of conscience builds into basic moral sensibility a quality not found in Kant. Conscience implies definite content and thus moves the discussion to the level of historical specificity. God watches over history and cannot be pleased with what human beings do to their fellow human beings.[26] Unlike Kant and Enlightenment culture generally, Niebuhr has a concrete historical consciousness and a dialectical imagination in which God appears over against the human as judge.

*　　*　　*

To conclude, the texts that follow propose a dialogue between Immanuel Kant and two twentieth-century theologians on the moral dimension of spirituality. We would like to emphasize the term "dialogue" as a way of drawing attention to the exploratory nature of associating these historical figures; while Kant, Tillich, and Niebuhr have much in common, considerable differences separate them. But, like Kant, the other two focus attention to the human subject as the place for encountering God. Both Tillich and Niebuhr follow Kant's turn to an analysis of subjectivity as the region of spiritual experience and ultimately encountering God. On that premise, we ask, how does sensibility for the good enter into the way human beings act in relation to what they take to be ultimate? The discussion is joined at a foundational level because, for all who consider the question, the answer will help determine who they are and what they wish to become.

Notes

1. Roger Scruton, *Kant* (Oxford: Oxford University Press, 1982), 14.

2. The term "transcendental" describes a universal structure of human consciousness as distinct from the term "transcendent," which refers to something that goes beyond all this-worldly reality.

3. Kant later wrote that "the remembrance of David Hume was the very thing that many years ago first interrupted my dogmatic slumber." *Prolegomena to Any Future Metaphysics*, trans. Gary Hatfield (Cambridge: Cambridge University Press, 1997; online 2001), 10.

4. Peter Gay, *The Enlightenment: An Interpretation* (New York: Knopf, 1966 & 1969), I, x.

5. Kant used the idea of daring to think or to know as the motto of the Enlightenment in his essay "Answering the Question: What Is Enlightenment?" written in 1784.

6. See Henry E. Allison, "Kant's Conception of Aufklärung," *Essays on Kant* (Oxford: Oxford University Press, 2012): 229–235.

7. Gay, *The Enlightenment*, I, 148.

8. Kant, *The Critique of Pure Reason*, trans. N. Kemp-Smith, cited by Scruton, *Kant*, 25.

9. Immanuel Kant, *Fundamental Principles of the Metaphysic of Morals*, trans. T. K. Abbott (Buffalo: Prometheus Books, 1988), 25.

10. For example, in Aquinas's Aristotelian ethics, an action is good because it advances the actor to his or her end of life and

fulfillment; in Calvin, one uses creatures well when they follow the intent or purpose written into the object by its creator; in consequentialism, an action is judged good by the consequences it aims at.

11. "A *maxim* is the subjective principle of volition. The objective principle . . . is the practical *law.*" Kant, *Fundamental Principles of the Metaphysic of Morals*, 25, n. 2; also, ibid., 49, n. 7.

12. Kant, *Fundamental Principles of the Metaphysic of Morals*, 27.

13. "But every other rational being regards its existence similarly, just on the same rational principle that holds for me, so that it is at the same time an objective principle, from which as a supreme practical law all laws of the will must be capable of being deduced." Ibid., 57–58.

14. The autonomy of the human person functions in Kant's thought in a way analogous to the absolute value of the human person, which operates in present-day Catholic moral teaching, although the parallelism is rarely alluded to. Note that this is a functional rather than a systematic analogy.

15. Scruton, *Kant*, 71–74.

16. Paul Tillich, *Morality and Beyond* (New York: Harper Torchbooks, 1963), 17–30.

17. Ibid., 22.

18. Ibid., 30.

19. Ibid., 24.

20. Ibid., 74. This opinion of Tillich occurs later in the book *Morality and Beyond*, but it is relevant to the view of Niebuhr on conscience.

21. Robin W. Lovin, *Christian Realism and the New Realities* (New York: Cambridge University Press, 2008), 93–95 at 94.

22. See, for example, John Henry Newman, *An Essay in Aid of a Grammar of Assent* (Notre Dame: University of Notre Dame Press, 1979), 97–107.

23. Reinhold Niebuhr, *The Nature and Destiny of Man, I. Human Nature* (New York: Charles Scribner's Sons, 1964), 127.

24. Ibid.

25. Ibid., 128.

26. Ibid., 132.

I

The Texts

[Immanuel Kant, "Preface," "First Section—Transition from the Common Rational Knowledge of Morality to the Philosophical," and selection from "Second Section—Transition from Popular Moral Philosophy to the Metaphysic of Morals," *Fundamental Principles of the Metaphysic of Morals*, trans. Thomas Kingsbill Abbott (Urbana, Ill.: Project Gutenberg).]

Preface

Ancient Greek philosophy was divided into three sciences: physics, ethics, and logic. This division is perfectly suitable to the nature of the thing; and the only improvement that can be made in it is to add the principle on which it is based, so that we may both satisfy ourselves of its completeness and also be able to determine correctly the necessary subdivisions.

All rational knowledge is either material or formal: the former considers some object; the latter is concerned only with the form of the understanding and of the reason itself, and with the universal laws of thought in general without distinction of its objects. Formal philosophy is called logic. Material philosophy, however, which has to do with determinate objects and the laws to which they are subject, is again twofold; for these laws are either laws of nature or of freedom. The science of the former is physics, that of the latter, ethics; they are also called natural philosophy and moral philosophy respectively.

21

Logic cannot have any empirical part; that is, a part in which the universal and necessary laws of thought should rest on grounds taken from experience; otherwise it would not be logic, i.e., a canon for the understanding or the reason, valid for all thought, and capable of demonstration. Natural and moral philosophy, on the contrary, can each have their empirical part, since the former has to determine the laws of nature as an object of experience; the latter the laws of the human will, so far as it is affected by nature: the former, however, being laws according to which everything does happen; the latter, laws according to which everything ought to happen. Ethics, however, must also consider the conditions under which what ought to happen frequently does not.

We may call all philosophy empirical, so far as it is based on grounds of experience: on the other hand, that which delivers its doctrines from *a priori* principles alone we may call pure philosophy. When the latter is merely formal it is logic; if it is restricted to definite objects of the understanding it is metaphysic.

In this way there arises the idea of a twofold metaphysic—a metaphysic of nature and a metaphysic of morals. Physics will thus have an empirical and also a rational part. It is the same with Ethics; but here the empirical part might have the special name of practical anthropology, the name morality being appropriated to the rational part.

All trades, arts, and handiworks have gained by division of labor, namely, when, instead of one man doing everything, each confines himself to a certain kind of work distinct from others in the treatment it requires, so as to be able to perform it with greater facility and in the greatest perfection. Where the different kinds of work are not distinguished and divided, where everyone is a jack-of-all-trades, there manufactures remain still in the greatest barbarism. It might deserve to be considered whether pure philosophy in all its parts does not require a man specially devoted to it, and whether it would not be better for the whole business of science if those who, to please the tastes of the public, are wont to blend the rational and empirical elements together, mixed in all sorts of proportions unknown to themselves, and who call themselves independent thinkers, giving the name of minute philosophers to those who apply themselves to the rational part only if these, I say, were warned not to carry on two employments together which differ widely in the treatment they demand, for each of which perhaps a special talent is required, and the combination of which in one person only produces bunglers. But I only ask here whether the nature of science does not require that we should always carefully separate the empirical from the rational part, and prefix to Physics proper (or empirical physics) a metaphysic of nature, and to practical anthropology a metaphysic of morals, which must be carefully cleared of everything empirical, so that we may know how much can be accomplished by pure reason in both cases, and from what sources it draws this its *a priori* teaching, and that whether the latter inquiry is conducted by all moralists (whose name is legion), or only by some who feel a calling thereto.

As my concern here is with moral philosophy, I limit the question suggested to this: Whether it is not of the utmost necessity to construct a pure thing which is only empirical and which belongs to anthropology? for that such a philosophy must be possible is evident from the common idea of duty and of the moral laws. Everyone must admit that if a law is to have moral force, i.e., to be the basis of an obligation, it must carry with it absolute necessity; that, for example, the precept, "Thou shalt not lie," is not valid for men alone, as if other rational beings had no need to observe it; and so with all the other moral laws properly so called; that, therefore, the basis of obligation must not be sought in the nature of man, or in the circumstances in the world in which he is placed, but *a priori* simply in the conception of pure reason; and although any other precept which is founded on principles of mere experience may be in certain respects universal, yet in as far as it rests even in the least degree on an empirical basis, perhaps only as to a motive, such a precept, while it may be a practical rule, can never be called a moral law.

Thus not only are moral laws with their principles essentially distinguished from every other kind of practical knowledge in which there is anything empirical, but all moral philosophy rests wholly on its pure part. When applied to man, it does not borrow the least thing from the knowledge of man himself (anthropology), but gives laws *a priori* to him as a rational being. No doubt these laws require a judgement sharpened by experience, in order on the one hand to distinguish in what cases they are applicable, and on the other to procure for them access to the will of the man and effectual influence on conduct; since man is acted on by so many inclinations that, though capable of the idea of a practical pure reason, he is not so easily able to make it effective *in concreto* in his life.

A metaphysic of morals is therefore indispensably necessary, not merely for speculative reasons, in order to investigate the sources of the practical principles which are to be found *a priori* in our reason, but also because morals themselves are liable to all sorts of corruption, as long as we are without that clue and supreme canon by which to estimate them correctly. For in order that an action should be morally good, it is not enough that it conform to the moral law, but it must also be done for the sake of the law, otherwise that conformity is only very contingent and uncertain; since a principle which is not moral, although it may now and then produce actions conformable to the law, will also often produce actions which contradict it. Now it is only in a pure philosophy that we can look for the moral law in its purity and genuineness (and, in a practical matter, this is of the utmost consequence): we must, therefore, begin with pure philosophy (metaphysic), and without it there cannot be any moral philosophy at all. That which mingles these pure principles with the empirical does not deserve the name of philosophy (for what distinguishes philosophy from common rational knowledge is that it treats in separate sciences what the latter only comprehends confusedly); much less does it deserve that of moral philosophy, since by this confusion it even spoils the purity of morals themselves, and counteracts its own end.

Let it not be thought, however, that what is here demanded is already extant in the propaedeutic prefixed by the celebrated Wolf to his moral philosophy, namely, his so-called general practical philosophy, and that, therefore, we have not to strike into an entirely new field. Just because it was to be a general practical philosophy, it has not taken into consideration a will of any particular kind—say one which should be determined solely from *a priori* principles without any empirical motives, and which we might call a pure will, but volition in general, with all the actions and conditions which belong to it in this general signification. By this it is distinguished from a metaphysic of morals, just as general logic, which treats of the acts and canons of thought in general, is distinguished from transcendental philosophy, which treats of the particular acts and canons of pure thought, i.e., that whose cognitions are altogether *a priori*. For the metaphysic of morals has to examine the idea and the principles of a possible pure will, and not the acts and conditions of human volition generally, which for the most part are drawn from psychology. It is true that moral laws and duty are spoken of in the general moral philosophy (contrary indeed to all fitness). But this is no objection, for in this respect also the authors of that science remain true to their idea of it; they do not distinguish the motives which are prescribed as such by reason alone altogether *a priori*, and which are properly moral, from the empirical motives which the understanding raises to general conceptions merely by comparison of experiences; but, without noticing the difference of their sources, and looking on them all as homogeneous, they consider only their greater or less amount. It is in this way they frame their notion of obligation, which, though anything but moral, is all that can be attained in a philosophy which passes no judgement at all on

the origin of all possible practical concepts, whether they are
a priori, or only *a posteriori*.

Intending to publish hereafter a metaphysic of morals, I
issue in the first instance these fundamental principles. Indeed
there is properly no other foundation for it than the critical
examination of a pure practical reason; just as that of metaphysics is the critical examination of the pure speculative
reason, already published. But in the first place the former is
not so absolutely necessary as the latter, because in moral
concerns human reason can easily be brought to a high degree
of correctness and completeness, even in the commonest understanding, while on the contrary in its theoretic but pure
use it is wholly dialectical; and in the second place if the critique
of a pure practical Reason is to be complete, it must be possible
at the same time to show its identity with the speculative reason
in a common principle, for it can ultimately be only one and
the same reason which has to be distinguished merely in its
application. I could not, however, bring it to such completeness
here, without introducing considerations of a wholly different
kind, which would be perplexing to the reader. On this account
I have adopted the title of Fundamental Principles of the
Metaphysic of Morals instead of that of a Critical Examination
of the pure practical reason.

But in the third place, since a metaphysic of morals, in spite
of the discouraging title, is yet capable of being presented in
popular form, and one adapted to the common understanding,
I find it useful to separate from it this preliminary treatise on
its fundamental principles, in order that I may not hereafter
have need to introduce these necessarily subtle discussions
into a book of a more simple character.

The present treatise is, however, nothing more than the
investigation and establishment of the supreme principle of
morality, and this alone constitutes a study complete in itself
and one which ought to be kept apart from every other moral
investigation. No doubt my conclusions on this weighty question, which has hitherto been very unsatisfactorily examined,

would receive much light from the application of the same principle to the whole system, and would be greatly confirmed by the adequacy which it exhibits throughout; but I must forgo this advantage, which indeed would be after all more gratifying than useful, since the easy applicability of a principle and its apparent adequacy give no very certain proof of its soundness, but rather inspire a certain partiality, which prevents us from examining and estimating it strictly in itself and without regard to consequences.

I have adopted in this work the method which I think most suitable, proceeding analytically from common knowledge to the determination of its ultimate principle, and again descending synthetically from the examination of this principle and its sources to the common knowledge in which we find it employed. The division will, therefore, be as follows:

1. FIRST SECTION. Transition from the common rational knowledge of morality to the philosophical.
2. SECOND SECTION. Transition from popular moral philosophy to the metaphysic of morals.
3. THIRD SECTION. Final step from the metaphysic of morals to the critique of the pure practical reason.

First Section — Transition from the Common Rational Knowledge of Morality to the Philosophical

Nothing can possibly be conceived in the world, or even out of it, which can be called good, without qualification, except a good will. Intelligence, wit, judgement, and the other talents of the mind, however they may be named, or courage, resolution, perseverance, as qualities of temperament, are undoubtedly good and desirable in many respects; but these gifts of nature may also become extremely bad and mischievous if the will which is to make use of them, and which, therefore, constitutes what is called character, is not good. It is the same with the gifts of fortune. Power, riches, honor, even health, and the general well-being and contentment with one's condition which is called happiness, inspire pride, and often presumption, if there is not a good will to correct the influence of these on the mind, and with this also to rectify the whole principle of acting and adapt it to its end. The sight of a being who is not adorned with a single feature of a pure and good will, enjoying unbroken prosperity, can never give pleasure to an impartial rational spectator. Thus a good will appears to constitute the indispensable condition even of being worthy of happiness.

There are even some qualities which are of service to this good will itself and may facilitate its action, yet which have no intrinsic unconditional value, but always presuppose a good will, and this qualifies the esteem that we justly have for them and does not permit us to regard them as absolutely good. Moderation in the affections and passions, self-control, and calm deliberation are not only good in many respects, but even seem to constitute part of the intrinsic worth of the person; but they are far from deserving to be called good without qualification, although they have been so unconditionally praised by the ancients. For without the principles of a good will, they may become extremely bad, and the coolness of a villain not only makes him far more dangerous, but also directly makes him more abominable in our eyes than he would have been without it.

A good will is good not because of what it performs or effects, not by its aptness for the attainment of some proposed end, but simply by virtue of the volition—that is, it is good in itself, and considered by itself is to be esteemed much higher than all that can be brought about by it in favor of any inclination, nay even of the sum total of all inclinations. Even if it should happen that, owing to special disfavor of fortune, or the niggardly provision of a step-motherly nature, this will should wholly lack power to accomplish its purpose, if with its greatest efforts it should yet achieve nothing, and there should remain only the good will (not, to be sure, a mere wish, but the summoning of all means in our power), then, like a jewel, it would still shine by its own light, as a thing which has its whole value in itself. Its usefulness or fruitlessness can neither add to nor take away anything from this value. It would be, as it were, only the setting to enable us to handle it the more conveniently in common commerce, or to attract to it the attention of those who are not yet connoisseurs, but not to recommend it to true connoisseurs, or to determine its value.

There is, however, something so strange in this idea of the absolute value of the mere will, in which no account is taken of its utility, that notwithstanding the thorough assent of even common reason to the idea, yet a suspicion must arise that it may perhaps really be the product of mere high-flown fancy, and that we may have misunderstood the purpose of nature in assigning reason as the governor of our will. Therefore we will examine this idea from this point of view.

In the physical constitution of an organized being—that is, a being adapted suitably to the purposes of life—we assume it as a fundamental principle that no organ for any purpose will be found but what is also the fittest and best adapted for that purpose. Now in a being which has reason and a will, if the proper object of nature were its conservation—its welfare, in a word, its happiness—then nature would have hit upon a very bad arrangement in selecting the reason of the creature to carry out this purpose. For all the actions which the creature has to perform with a view to this purpose, and the whole rule of its conduct, would be far more surely prescribed to it by instinct, and that end would have been attained thereby much more certainly than it ever can be by reason. Should reason have been communicated to this favored creature over and above, it must only have served it to contemplate the happy constitution of its nature, to admire it, to congratulate itself thereon, and to feel thankful for it to the beneficent cause, but not that it should subject its desires to that weak and delusive guidance and meddle bunglingly with the purpose of nature. In a word, nature would have taken care that reason should not break forth into practical exercise, nor have the presumption, with its weak insight, to think out for itself the plan of happiness, and of the means of attaining it. Nature would not only have taken on herself the choice of the ends, but also of the means, and with wise foresight would have entrusted both to instinct.

And, in fact, we find that the more a cultivated reason applies itself with deliberate purpose to the enjoyment of life and happiness, so much the more does the man fail of true satisfaction. And from this circumstance there arises in many, if they are candid enough to confess it, a certain degree of misology—that is, hatred of reason, especially in the case of those who are most experienced in the use of it—because after calculating all the advantages they derive, I do not say from the invention of all the arts of common luxury, but even from the sciences (which seem to them to be after all only a luxury of the understanding), they find that they have, in fact, only brought more trouble on their shoulders, rather than gained in happiness; and they end by envying, rather than despising, the more common stamp of men who keep closer to the guidance of mere instinct and do not allow their reason much influence on their conduct. And this we must admit, that the judgement of those who would very much lower the lofty eulogies of the advantages which reason gives us in regard to the happiness and satisfaction of life, or who would even reduce them below zero, is by no means morose or ungrateful to the goodness with which the world is governed, but that there lies at the root of these judgements the idea that our existence has a different and far nobler end, for which, and not for happiness, reason is properly intended, and which must, therefore, be regarded as the supreme condition to which the private ends of man must, for the most part, be postponed.

For as reason is not competent to guide the will with certainty in regard to its objects and the satisfaction of all our wants (which it to some extent even multiplies), this being an end to which an implanted instinct would have led with much greater certainty; and since, nevertheless, reason is imparted to us as a practical faculty, i.e., as one which is to have influence on the will, therefore, admitting that nature generally in the distribution of her capacities has adapted the means to the end, its true destination must be to produce a will, not merely good as a means to something else, but good in itself, for which reason was absolutely necessary. This will, then, though not indeed the sole and complete good, must be the supreme good and the condition of every other, even of the desire of happiness. Under these circumstances, there is nothing inconsistent with the wisdom of nature in the fact that the cultivation of the reason, which is requisite for the first and unconditional purpose, does in many ways interfere, at least in this life, with the attainment of the second, which is always conditional, namely, happiness. Nay, it may even reduce it to nothing, without nature thereby failing of her purpose. For reason recognizes the establishment of a good will as its highest practical destination, and in attaining this purpose is capable only of a satisfaction of its own proper kind, namely that from the attainment of an end, which end again is determined by reason only, notwithstanding that this may involve many a disappointment to the ends of inclination.

We have then to develop the notion of a will which deserves to be highly esteemed for itself and is good without a view to anything further, a notion which exists already in the sound natural understanding, requiring rather to be cleared up than to be taught, and which in estimating the value of our actions always takes the first place and constitutes the condition of all the rest. In order to do this, we will take the notion of duty, which includes that of a good will, although implying certain subjective restrictions and hindrances. These, however, far from concealing it, or rendering it unrecognizable, rather bring it out by contrast and make it shine forth so much the brighter.

I omit here all actions which are already recognized as inconsistent with duty, although they may be useful for this or that purpose, for with these the question of whether they are done from duty cannot arise at all, since they even conflict with it. I also set aside those actions which really conform to duty, but to which men have no direct inclination, performing them because they are impelled thereto by some other inclination. For in this case we can readily distinguish whether the action which agrees with duty is done from duty, or from a selfish view. It is much harder to make this distinction when the action accords with duty and the subject has besides a direct inclination to it. For example, it is always a matter of duty that a dealer should not over charge an inexperienced purchaser; and wherever there is much commerce the prudent tradesman does not overcharge, but keeps a fixed price for everyone, so that a child buys of him as well as any other. Men are thus honestly served; but this is not enough to make us believe that the tradesman has so acted from duty and from principles of honesty: his own advantage required it; it is out of the question in this case to suppose that he might besides have a direct inclination in favor of the buyers, so that, as it were, from love he should give no advantage to one over another. Accordingly the action was done neither from duty nor from direct inclination, but merely with a selfish view.

On the other hand, it is a duty to maintain one's life; and, in addition, everyone has also a direct inclination to do so. But on this account the often anxious care which most men take for it has no intrinsic worth, and their maxim has no moral import. They preserve their life as duty requires, no doubt, but not because duty requires. On the other hand, if adversity and hopeless sorrow have completely taken away the relish for life; if the unfortunate one, strong in mind, indignant at his fate rather than desponding or dejected, wishes for death, and yet preserves his life without loving it—not from inclination or fear, but from duty—then his maxim has a moral worth.

To be beneficent when we can is a duty; and besides this, there are many minds so sympathetically constituted that, without any other motive of vanity or self-interest, they find a pleasure in spreading joy around them and can take delight in the satisfaction of others so far as it is their own work. But I maintain that in such a case an action of this kind, however proper, however amiable it may be, has nevertheless no true moral worth, but is on a level with other inclinations, e.g., the inclination to honor, which, if it is happily directed to that which is in fact of public utility and accordant with duty and consequently honorable, deserves praise and encouragement, but not esteem. For the maxim lacks the moral import, namely, that such actions be done from duty, not from inclination. Put the case that the mind of that philanthropist were clouded by sorrow of his own, extinguishing all sympathy with the lot of others, and that, while he still has the power to benefit others in distress, he is not touched by their trouble because he is absorbed with his own; and now suppose that he tears himself out of this dead insensibility, and performs the action without any inclination to it, but simply from duty, then first has his action its genuine moral worth. Further still; if nature has put little sympathy in the heart of this or that man; if he, supposed to be an upright man, is by temperament cold and indifferent to the sufferings of others, perhaps because in respect of his own he is provided with the special gift of patience and fortitude and supposes, or even requires, that others should have the same—and such a man would certainly not be the meanest product of nature—but if nature had not specially framed him for a philanthropist, would he not still find in himself a source from whence to give himself a far higher worth than that of a good-natured temperament could be? Unquestionably. It is just in this that the moral worth of the character is brought out which is incomparably the highest of all, namely, that he is beneficent, not from inclination, but from duty.

To secure one's own happiness is a duty, at least indirectly; for discontent with one's condition, under a pressure of many anxieties and amidst unsatisfied wants, might easily become a great temptation to transgression of duty. But here again, without looking to duty, all men have already the strongest and most intimate inclination to happiness, because it is just in this idea that all inclinations are combined in one total. But the precept of happiness is often of such a sort that it greatly interferes with some inclinations, and yet a man cannot form any definite and certain conception of the sum of satisfaction of all of them which is called happiness. It is not then to be wondered at that a single inclination, definite both as to what it promises and as to the time within which it can be gratified, is often able to overcome such a fluctuating idea, and that a gouty patient, for instance, can choose to enjoy what he likes, and to suffer what he may, since, according to his calculation, on this occasion at least, he has not sacrificed the enjoyment of the present moment to a possibly mistaken expectation of a happiness which is supposed to be found in health. But even in this case, if the general desire for happiness did not influence his will, and supposing that in his particular case health was not a necessary element in this calculation, there yet remains in this, as in all other cases, this law, namely, that he should promote his happiness not from inclination but from duty, and by this would his conduct first acquire true moral worth.

It is in this manner, undoubtedly, that we are to understand those passages of Scripture also in which we are commanded to love our neighbor, even our enemy. For love, as an affection, cannot be commanded, but beneficence for duty's sake may; even though we are not impelled to it by any inclination—nay, are even repelled by a natural and unconquerable aversion. This is practical love and not pathological—a love which is seated in the will, and not in the propensions of sense—in principles of action and not of tender sympathy; and it is this love alone which can be commanded.

The second proposition is: That an action done from duty derives its moral worth, not from the purpose which is to be attained by it, but from the maxim by which it is determined, and therefore does not depend on the realization of the object of the action, but merely on the principle of volition by which the action has taken place, without regard to any object of desire. It is clear from what precedes that the purposes which we may have in view in our actions, or their effects regarded as ends and springs of the will, cannot give to actions any unconditional or moral worth. In what, then, can their worth lie, if it is not to consist in the will and in reference to its expected effect? It cannot lie anywhere but in the principle of the will without regard to the ends which can be attained by the action. For the will stands between its *a priori* principle, which is formal, and its *a posteriori* spring, which is material, as between two roads, and as it must be determined by something, it follows that it must be determined by the formal principle of volition when an action is done from duty, in which case every material principle has been withdrawn from it.

The third proposition, which is a consequence of the two preceding, I would express thus: Duty is the necessity of acting from respect for the law. I may have inclination for an object as the effect of my proposed action, but I cannot have respect for it, just for this reason, that it is an effect and not an energy of will. Similarly I cannot have respect for inclination, whether my own or another's; I can at most, if my own, approve it; if another's, sometimes even love it; i.e., look on it as favorable to my own interest. It is only what is connected with my will as a principle, by no means as an effect—what does not subserve my inclination, but overpowers it, or at least in case of choice excludes it from its calculation—in other words, simply the law of itself, which can be an object of respect, and hence a command. Now an action done from duty must wholly

exclude the influence of inclination and with it every object
of the will, so that nothing remains which can determine the
will except objectively the law, and subjectively pure respect
for this practical law, and consequently the maxim[1] that I
should follow this law even to the thwarting of all my
inclinations.

Thus the moral worth of an action does not lie in the effect
expected from it, nor in any principle of action which requires
to borrow its motive from this expected effect. For all these
effects—agreeableness of one's condition and even the promotion of the happiness of others—could have been also
brought about by other causes, so that for this there would
have been no need of the will of a rational being; whereas it
is in this alone that the supreme and unconditional good can
be found. The pre-eminent good which we call moral can
therefore consist in nothing else than the conception of law
in itself, which certainly is only possible in a rational being,
in so far as this conception, and not the expected effect, determines the will. This is a good which is already present in
the person who acts accordingly, and we have not to wait for
it to appear first in the result.[2]

But what sort of law can that be, the conception of which
must determine the will, even without paying any regard to
the effect expected from it, in order that this will may be called
good absolutely and without qualification? As I have deprived
the will of every impulse which could arise to it from obedience to any law, there remains nothing but the universal
conformity of its actions to law in general, which alone is to
serve the will as a principle, i.e., I am never to act otherwise
than so that I could also will that my maxim should become
a universal law. Here, now, it is the simple conformity to law
in general, without assuming any particular law applicable
to certain actions, that serves the will as its principle and must
so serve it, if duty is not to be a vain delusion and a chimerical
notion. The common reason of men in its practical judgements perfectly coincides with this and always has in view

the principle here suggested. Let the question be, for example: May I when in distress make a promise with the intention not to keep it? I readily distinguish here between the two signifi-cations which the question may have: Whether it is prudent, or whether it is right, to make a false promise? The former may undoubtedly often be the case. I see clearly indeed that it is not enough to extricate myself from a present difficulty by means of this subterfuge, but it must be well considered whether there may not hereafter spring from this lie much greater inconvenience than that from which I now free myself, and as, with all my supposed cunning, the consequences cannot be so easily foreseen but that credit once lost may be much more injurious to me than any mischief which I seek to avoid at present, it should be considered whether it would not be more prudent to act herein according to a universal maxim and to make it a habit to promise nothing except with the intention of keeping it. But it is soon clear to me that such a maxim will still only be based on the fear of consequences. Now it is a wholly different thing to be truthful from duty and to be so from apprehension of injurious consequences. In the first case, the very notion of the action already implies a law for me; in the second case, I must first look about else-where to see what results may be combined with it which would affect myself. For to deviate from the principle of duty is beyond all doubt wicked; but to be unfaithful to my maxim of prudence may often be very advantageous to me, although to abide by it is certainly safer. The shortest way, however, and an unerring one, to discover the answer to this question whether a lying promise is consistent with duty, is to ask myself, "Should I be content that my maxim (to extricate myself from difficulty by a false promise) should hold good as a universal law, for myself as well as for others?" and should I be able to say to myself, "Every one may make a deceitful promise when he finds himself in a difficulty from which he cannot otherwise extricate himself"? Then I presently become aware that while I can will the lie, I can by no means will that lying should be a universal law. For with such a law there would be no promises at all, since it would be in vain to allege my intention in regard to my future actions to those who would not believe this allegation, or if they over hastily did so would pay me back in my own coin. Hence my maxim, as soon as it should be made a universal law, would necessarily destroy itself.

I do not, therefore, need any far-reaching penetration to discern what I have to do in order that my will may be morally good. Inexperienced in the course of the world, incapable of being prepared for all its contingencies, I only ask myself: Canst thou also will that thy maxim should be a universal law? If not, then it must be rejected, and that not because of a disadvantage accruing from it to myself or even to others, but because it cannot enter as a principle into a possible universal legislation, and reason extorts from me immediate respect for such legislation. I do not indeed as yet discern on what this respect is based (this the philosopher may inquire), but at least I understand this, that it is an estimation of the worth which far outweighs all worth of what is recommended by inclination, and that the necessity of acting from pure respect for the practical law is what constitutes duty, to which every other motive must give place, because it is the condition of a will being good in itself, and the worth of such a will is above everything.

Thus, then, without quitting the moral knowledge of common human reason, we have arrived at its principle. And although, no doubt, common men do not conceive it in such an abstract and universal form, yet they always have it really before their eyes and use it as the standard of their decision. Here it would be easy to show how, with this compass in hand, men are well able to distinguish, in every case that occurs, what is good, what bad, conformably to duty or inconsistent with it, if, without in the least teaching them anything new, we only, like Socrates, direct their attention to the principle they themselves employ; and that, therefore, we do not need science and philosophy to know what we should do to be honest and good, yea, even wise and virtuous. Indeed we might well have conjectured beforehand that the knowledge of what every man is bound to do, and therefore also to know, would be within the reach of every man, even the commonest. Here we cannot forbear admiration when we see how great an advantage the practical judgement has over the theoretical in the common understanding of men. In the latter, if common reason ventures to depart from the laws of experience and from the perceptions of the senses, it falls into mere inconceivabilities and self-contradictions, at least into a chaos of uncertainty, obscurity, and instability. But in the practical sphere it is just when the common understanding excludes all sensible springs from practical laws that its power of judgement begins to show itself to advantage. It then becomes even subtle, whether it be that it chicanes with its own conscience or with other claims respecting what is to be called right, or whether it desires for its own instruction to determine honestly the worth of actions; and, in the latter case, it may even have as good a hope of hitting the mark as any philosopher whatever can promise himself. Nay, it is almost more sure of doing so, because the philosopher cannot have any other principle, while he may easily perplex his judgement by a multitude of considerations foreign to the matter, and so turn aside from the right way. Would it not therefore be wiser in moral concerns to acquiesce in the judgement of common reason, or at most only to call in philosophy for the purpose of rendering the system of morals more complete and intelligible, and its rules more convenient for use (especially for disputation), but not so as to draw off the common understanding from its happy simplicity, or to bring it by means of philosophy into a new path of inquiry and instruction?

Innocence is indeed a glorious thing; only, on the other hand, it is very sad that it cannot well maintain itself and is easily seduced. On this account even wisdom—which otherwise consists more in conduct than in knowledge—yet has need of science, not in order to learn from it, but to secure for its precepts admission and permanence. Against all the commands of duty which reason represents to man as so deserving of respect, he feels in himself a powerful counterpoise in his wants and inclinations, the entire satisfaction of which he sums up under the name of happiness. Now reason issues its commands unyieldingly, without promising anything to the inclinations, and, as it were, with disregard and contempt for these claims, which are so impetuous, and at the same time so plausible, and which will not allow themselves to be suppressed by any command. Hence there arises a natural dialectic, i.e., a disposition, to argue against these strict laws of duty and to question their validity, or at least their purity and strictness; and, if possible, to make them more accordant with our wishes and inclinations, that is to say, to corrupt them at their very source, and entirely to destroy their worth—a thing which even common practical reason cannot ultimately call good.

Thus is the common reason of man compelled to go out of its sphere, and to take a step into the field of a practical philosophy, not to satisfy any speculative want (which never occurs to it as long as it is content to be mere sound reason), but even on practical grounds, in order to attain in it information and clear instruction respecting the source of its principle, and the correct determination of it in opposition to the maxims which are based on wants and inclinations, so that it may escape from the perplexity of opposite claims and not run the risk of losing all genuine moral principles through the equivocation into which it easily falls. Thus, when practical reason cultivates itself, there insensibly arises in it a dialectic which forces it to seek aid in philosophy, just as happens to it in its theoretic use; and in this case, therefore, as well as in the other, it will find rest nowhere but in a thorough critical examination of our reason.

Selection from Second Section—Transition from Popular Moral Philosophy to the Metaphysic of Morals

Such a metaphysic of morals, completely isolated, not mixed with any anthropology, theology, physics, or hyperphysics, and still less with occult qualities (which we might call hypophysical), is not only an indispensable substratum of all sound theoretical knowledge of duties, but is at the same time a desideratum of the highest importance to the actual fulfillment of their precepts. For the pure conception of duty, unmixed with any foreign addition of empirical attractions, and, in a word, the conception of the moral law, exercises on the human heart, by way of reason alone (which first becomes aware with this that it can of itself be practical), an influence so much more powerful than all other springs[3] which may be derived from the field of experience, that, in the consciousness of its worth, it despises the latter, and can by degrees become their master; whereas a mixed ethics, compounded partly of motives drawn from feelings and inclinations, and partly also of conceptions of reason, must make the mind waver between motives which cannot be brought under any principle, which lead to good only by mere accident and very often also to evil.

From what has been said, it is clear that all moral conceptions have their seat and origin completely *a priori* in the reason, and that, moreover, in the commonest reason just as truly as in that which is in the highest degree speculative; that they cannot be obtained by abstraction from any empirical, and therefore merely contingent, knowledge; that it is just this purity of their origin that makes them worthy to serve as our supreme practical principle, and that just in proportion as we add anything empirical, we detract from their genuine influence and from the absolute value of actions; that it is not only of the greatest necessity, in a purely speculative point of view, but is also of the greatest practical importance, to derive these notions and laws from pure reason, to present them pure and unmixed, and even to determine the compass of this practical or pure rational knowledge, i.e., to determine the whole faculty of pure practical reason; and, in doing so, we must not make its principles dependent on the particular nature of human reason, though in speculative philosophy this may be permitted, or may even at times be necessary; but since moral laws ought to hold good for every rational creature, we must derive them from the general concept of a rational being. In this way, although for its application to man morality has need of anthropology, yet, in the first instance, we must treat it independently as pure philosophy, i.e., as metaphysic, complete in itself (a thing which in such distinct branches of science is easily done); knowing well that unless we are in possession of this, it would not only be vain to determine the moral element of duty in right actions for purposes of speculative criticism, but it would be impossible to base morals on their genuine principles, even for common practical purposes, especially of moral instruction, so as to produce pure moral dispositions, and to engraft them on men's minds to the promotion of the greatest possible good in the world.

But in order that in this study we may not merely advance by the natural steps from the common moral judgement (in this case very worthy of respect) to the philosophical, as has been already done, but also from a popular philosophy, which goes no further than it can reach by groping with the help of examples, to metaphysic (which does allow itself to be checked by anything empirical and, as it must measure the whole extent of this kind of rational knowledge, goes as far as ideal conceptions, where even examples fail us), we must follow and clearly describe the practical faculty of reason, from the general rules of its determination to the point where the notion of duty springs from it.

Everything in nature works according to laws. Rational beings alone have the faculty of acting according to the conception of laws, that is according to principles, i.e., have a will.

Since the deduction of actions from principles requires reason, the will is nothing but practical reason. If reason infallibly determines the will, then the actions of such a being which are recognized as objectively necessary are subjectively necessary also, i.e., the will is a faculty to choose that only which reason independent of inclination recognizes as practically necessary, i.e., as good. But if reason of itself does not sufficiently determine the will, if the latter is subject also to subjective conditions (particular impulses) which do not always coincide with the objective conditions; in a word, if the will does not in itself completely accord with reason (which is actually the case with men), then the actions which objectively are recognized as necessary are subjectively contingent, and the determination of such a will according to objective laws is obligation, that is to say, the relation of the objective laws to a will that is not thoroughly good is conceived as the determination of the will of a rational being by principles of reason, but which the will from its nature does not of necessity follow.

The conception of an objective principle, in so far as it is obligatory for a will, is called a command (of reason), and the formula of the command is called an imperative.

All imperatives are expressed by the word *ought* [or *shall*], and thereby indicate the relation of an objective law of reason to a will, which from its subjective constitution is not necessarily determined by it (an obligation). They say that something would be good to do or to forbear, but they say it to a will which does not always do a thing because it is conceived to be good to do it. That is practically good, however, which determines the will by means of the conceptions of reason, and consequently not from subjective causes, but objectively, that is on principles which are valid for every rational being as such. It is distinguished from the pleasant, as that which influences the will only by means of sensation from merely subjective causes, valid only for the sense of this or that one, and not as a principle of reason, which holds for everyone.[4]

A perfectly good will would therefore be equally subject to objective laws (viz., laws of good), but could not be conceived as obliged thereby to act lawfully, because of itself from its subjective constitution it can only be determined by the conception of good. Therefore no imperatives hold for the Divine will, or in general for a holy will; *ought* is here out of place, because the volition is already of itself necessarily in unison with the law. Therefore imperatives are only formulae to express the relation of objective laws of all volition to the subjective imperfection of the will of this or that rational being, e.g., the human will.

Now all imperatives command either hypothetically or categorically. The former represent the practical necessity of a possible action as a means to something else that is willed (or at least which one might possibly will). The categorical imperative would be that which represented an action as necessary of itself without reference to another end, i.e., as objectively necessary.

Since every practical law represents a possible action as good and, on this account, for a subject who is practically determinable by reason, necessary, all imperatives are formulae determining an action which is necessary according to the principle of a will good in some respects. If now the action is good only as a means to something else, then the imperative is hypothetical; if it is conceived as good in itself and consequently as being necessarily the principle of a will which of itself conforms to reason, then it is categorical.

Thus the imperative declares what action possible by me would be good and presents the practical rule in relation to a will which does not forthwith perform an action simply because it is good, whether because the subject does not always know that it is good, or because, even if it know this, yet its maxims might be opposed to the objective principles of practical reason.

Accordingly the hypothetical imperative only says that the action is good for some purpose, possible or actual. In the first case it is a problematical, in the second an assertorial practical principle. The categorical imperative which declares an action to be objectively necessary in itself without reference to any purpose, i.e., without any other end, is valid as an apodictic (practical) principle.

Whatever is possible only by the power of some rational being may also be conceived as a possible purpose of some will; and therefore the principles of action as regards the means necessary to attain some possible purpose are in fact infinitely numerous. All sciences have a practical part, consisting of problems expressing that some end is possible for us and of imperatives directing how it may be attained. These may, therefore, be called in general imperatives of skill. Here there is no question whether the end is rational and good, but only what one must do in order to attain it. The precepts for the physician to make his patient thoroughly healthy, and for a poisoner to ensure certain death, are of equal value in this respect, that each serves to effect its purpose perfectly. Since in early youth it cannot be known what ends are likely to occur to us in the course of life, parents seek to have their children taught a great many things, and provide for their skill in the use of means for all sorts of arbitrary ends, of none of which can they determine whether it may not perhaps hereafter be an object to their pupil, but which it is at all events possible that he might aim at; and this anxiety is so great that they commonly neglect to form and correct their judgement on the value of the things which may be chosen as ends.

There is one end, however, which may be assumed to be actually such to all rational beings (so far as imperatives apply to them, viz., as dependent beings), and, therefore, one purpose which they not merely may have, but which we may with certainty assume that they all actually have by a natural necessity, and this is happiness. The hypothetical imperative which expresses the practical necessity of an action as means to the advancement of happiness is assertorial. We are not to present it as necessary for an uncertain and merely possible purpose, but for a purpose which we may presuppose with certainty and *a priori* exists in every man, because it belongs to his being. Now skill in the choice of means to his own greatest well-being may be called prudence,[5] in the narrowest sense. And thus the imperative which refers to the choice of means to one's own happiness, i.e., the precept of prudence, is still always hypothetical; the action is not commanded absolutely, but only as means to another purpose.

Finally, there is an imperative which commands a certain conduct immediately, without having as its condition any other purpose to be attained by it. This imperative is categorical. It concerns not the matter of the action, or its intended result, but its form and the principle of which it is itself a result; and what is essentially good in it consists in the mental disposition, let the consequence be what it may. This imperative may be called that of morality.

There is a marked distinction also between the volitions on these three sorts of principles in the dissimilarity of the obligation of the will. In order to mark this difference more clearly, I think they would be most suitably named in their order if we said they are either rules of skill, or counsels of prudence, or commands (laws) of morality. For it is law only that involves the conception of an unconditional and objective necessity, which is consequently universally valid; and commands are laws which must be obeyed, that is, must be followed, even in opposition to inclination. Counsels, indeed, involve necessity, but one which can only hold under a contingent subjective condition, viz., they depend on whether this or that man reckons this or that as part of his happiness; the categorical imperative, on the contrary, is not limited by any condition, and as being absolutely, although practically, necessary, may be quite properly called a command. We might also call the first kind of imperatives technical (belonging to art), the second pragmatic[6] (to welfare), the third moral (belonging to free conduct generally, that is, to morals).

Now arises the question, how are all these imperatives possible? This question does not seek to know how we can conceive the accomplishment of the action which the imperative ordains, but merely how we can conceive the obligation of the will which the imperative expresses. No special explanation is needed to show how an imperative of skill is possible. Whoever wills the end, wills also (so far as reason decides his conduct) the means in his power which are indispensably necessary thereto. This proposition is, as regards the volition, analytical; for, in willing an object as my effect, there is already thought the causality of myself as an acting cause, that is to say, the use of the means; and the imperative educes from the conception of volition of an end the conception of actions necessary to this end. Synthetical propositions must no doubt be employed in defining the means to a proposed end; but they do not concern the principle, the act of the will, but the object and its realization. E.g., that in order to bisect a line on an unerring principle I must draw from its extremities two intersecting arcs; this no doubt is taught by mathematics only in synthetical propositions; but if I know that it is only by this process that the intended operation can be performed, then to say that, if I fully will the operation, I also will the action required for it, is an analytical proposition; for it is one and the same thing to conceive something as an effect which I can produce in a certain way, and to conceive myself as acting in this way.

If it were only equally easy to give a definite conception of happiness, the imperatives of prudence would correspond exactly with those of skill, and would likewise be analytical. For in this case as in that, it could be said: "Whoever wills the end, wills also (according to the dictate of reason necessarily) the indispensable means thereto which are in his power." But, unfortunately, the notion of happiness is so indefinite that although every man wishes to attain it, yet he never can say definitely and consistently what it is that he really wishes and wills. The reason of this is that all the elements which belong to the notion of happiness are altogether empirical, i.e., they must be borrowed from experience, and nevertheless the idea of happiness requires an absolute whole, a maximum of welfare in my present and all future circumstances. Now it is impossible that the most clear-sighted and at the same time most powerful being (supposed finite) should frame to himself a definite conception of what he really wills in this. Does he will riches, how much anxiety, envy, and snares might he not thereby draw upon his shoulders? Does he will knowledge and discernment, perhaps it might prove to be only an eye so much the sharper to show him so much the more fearfully the evils that are now concealed from him, and that cannot be avoided, or to impose more wants on his desires, which already give him concern enough. Would he have long life? who guarantees to him that it would not be a long misery? would he at least have health? how often has uneasiness of the body restrained from excesses into which perfect health would have allowed one to fall? and so on. In short, he is unable, on any principle, to determine with certainty what would make him truly happy; because to do so he would need to be omniscient. We cannot therefore act on any definite principles to secure happiness, but only on empirical counsels, e.g. of regimen, frugality, courtesy, reserve, etc., which experience teaches do, on the average, most promote well-being. Hence it follows that the imperatives of prudence do not, strictly speaking, command at all, that is, they cannot present actions objectively as practically necessary; that they are rather to be regarded as counsels (*consilia*) than precepts of reason, that the problem to determine certainly and universally what action would promote the happiness of a rational being is completely insoluble, and consequently no imperative respecting it is possible which should, in the strict sense, command to do what makes happy; because happiness is not an ideal of reason but of imagination, resting solely on empirical grounds, and it is vain to expect that these should define an action by which one could attain the totality of a series of consequences which is really endless. This imperative of prudence would however be an analytical proposition if we assume that the means to happiness could be certainly assigned; for it is distinguished from the imperative of skill only by this, that in the latter the end is merely possible, in the former it is given; as however both only ordain the means to that which we suppose to be willed as an end, it follows that the imperative which ordains the willing of the means to him who wills the end is in both cases analytical. Thus there is no difficulty in regard to the possibility of an imperative of this kind either.

On the other hand, the question how the imperative of morality is possible, is undoubtedly one, the only one, demanding a solution, as this is not at all hypothetical, and the objective necessity which it presents cannot rest on any hypothesis, as is the case with the hypothetical imperatives. Only here we must never leave out of consideration that we cannot make out by any example, in other words empirically, whether there is such an imperative at all, but it is rather to be feared that all those which seem to be categorical may yet be at bottom hypothetical. For instance, when the precept is: "Thou shalt not promise deceitfully"; and it is assumed that the necessity of this is not a mere counsel to avoid some other evil, so that it should mean: "Thou shalt not make a lying promise, lest if it become known thou shouldst destroy thy credit," but that an action of this kind must be regarded as evil in itself, so that the imperative of the prohibition is categorical; then we cannot show with certainty in any example that the will was determined merely by the law, without any other spring of action, although it may appear to be so. For it is always possible that fear of disgrace, perhaps also obscure dread of other dangers, may have a secret influence on the will. Who can prove by experience the non-existence of a cause when all that experience tells us is that we do not perceive it? But in such a case the so-called moral imperative, which as such appears to be categorical and unconditional, would in reality be only a pragmatic precept, drawing our attention to our own interests and merely teaching us to take these into consideration.

We shall therefore have to investigate *a priori* the possibility of a categorical imperative, as we have not in this case the advantage of its reality being given in experience, so that [the elucidation of] its possibility should be requisite only for its explanation, not for its establishment. In the meantime it may be discerned beforehand that the categorical imperative alone has the purport of a practical law; all the rest may indeed be called principles of the will but not laws, since whatever is only necessary for the attainment of some arbitrary purpose may be considered as in itself contingent, and we can at any time be free from the precept if we give up the purpose; on the contrary, the unconditional command leaves the will no liberty to choose the opposite; consequently it alone carries with it that necessity which we require in a law.

Secondly, in the case of this categorical imperative or law of morality, the difficulty (of discerning its possibility) is a very profound one. It is an *a priori* synthetical practical proposition;[7] and as there is so much difficulty in discerning the possibility of speculative propositions of this kind, it may readily be supposed that the difficulty will be no less with the practical.

In this problem we will first inquire whether the mere conception of a categorical imperative may not perhaps supply us also with the formula of it, containing the proposition which alone can be a categorical imperative; for even if we know the tenor of such an absolute command, yet how it is possible will require further special and laborious study, which we postpone to the last section.

When I conceive a hypothetical imperative, in general I do not know beforehand what it will contain until I am given the condition. But when I conceive a categorical imperative, I know at once what it contains. For as the imperative contains besides the law only the necessity that the maxims[8] shall conform to this law, while the law contains no conditions restricting it, there remains nothing but the general statement that the maxim of the action should conform to a universal law, and it is this conformity alone that the imperative properly represents as necessary.

There is therefore but one categorical imperative, namely, this: Act only on that maxim whereby thou canst at the same time will that it should become a universal law.

Now if all imperatives of duty can be deduced from this one imperative as from their principle, then, although it should remain undecided what is called duty is not merely a vain notion, yet at least we shall be able to show what we understand by it and what this notion means.

Since the universality of the law according to which effects are produced constitutes what is properly called nature in the most general sense (as to form), that is the existence of things so far as it is determined by general laws, the imperative of duty may be expressed thus: Act as if the maxim of thy action were to become by thy will a universal law of nature.

We will now enumerate a few duties, adopting the usual division of them into duties to ourselves and to others, and into perfect and imperfect duties.[9]

   1. A man reduced to despair by a series of misfortunes feels wearied of life, but is still so far in possession of his reason that he can ask himself whether it would not be contrary to his duty to himself to take his own life. Now he inquires whether the maxim of his action could become a universal law of nature. His maxim is: "From self-love I adopt it as a principle to shorten my life when its longer duration is likely to bring more evil than satisfaction." It is asked then simply whether this principle founded on self-love can become a universal law of nature. Now we see at once that a system of nature of which it should be a law to destroy life by means of the very feeling whose special nature it is to impel

to the improvement of life would contradict itself
and, therefore, could not exist as a system of
nature; hence that maxim cannot possibly exist as
a universal law of nature and, consequently, would
be wholly inconsistent with the supreme principle
of all duty.

2. Another finds himself forced by necessity to
borrow money. He knows that he will not be able
to repay it, but sees also that nothing will be lent
to him unless he promises stoutly to repay it in a
definite time. He desires to make this promise, but
he has still so much conscience as to ask himself:
"Is it not unlawful and inconsistent with duty to
get out of a difficulty in this way?" Suppose
however that he resolves to do so: then the maxim
of his action would be expressed thus: "When I
think myself in want of money, I will borrow
money and promise to repay it, although I know
that I never can do so." Now this principle of
self-love or of one's own advantage may perhaps
be consistent with my whole future welfare; but
the question now is, "Is it right?" I change then the
suggestion of self-love into a universal law, and
state the question thus: "How would it be if my
maxim were a universal law?" Then I see at once
that it could never hold as a universal law of
nature, but would necessarily contradict itself. For
supposing it to be a universal law that everyone
when he thinks himself in a difficulty should be
able to promise whatever he pleases, with the
purpose of not keeping his promise, the promise
itself would become impossible, as well as the end
that one might have in view in it, since no one
would consider that anything was promised to
him, but would ridicule all such statements as vain
pretenses.

3. A third finds in himself a talent which with the help of some culture might make him a useful man in many respects. But he finds himself in comfortable circumstances and prefers to indulge in pleasure rather than to take pains in enlarging and improving his happy natural capacities. He asks, however, whether his maxim of neglect of his natural gifts, besides agreeing with his inclination to indulgence, agrees also with what is called duty. He sees then that a system of nature could indeed subsist with such a universal law although men (like the South Sea islanders) should let their talents rest and resolve to devote their lives merely to idleness, amusement, and propagation of their species—in a word, to enjoyment—but he cannot possibly will that this should be a universal law of nature, or be implanted in us as such by a natural instinct. For, as a rational being, he necessarily wills that his faculties be developed, since they serve him and have been given him, for all sorts of possible purposes.

4. A fourth, who is in prosperity, while he sees that others have to contend with great wretchedness and that he could help them, thinks: "What concern is it of mine? Let everyone be as happy as Heaven pleases, or as he can make himself; I will take nothing from him nor even envy him, only I do not wish to contribute anything to his welfare or to his assistance in distress!" Now no doubt if such a mode of thinking were a universal law, the human race might very well subsist and doubtless even better than in a state in which everyone talks of sympathy and good-will, or even takes care occasionally to put it into practice, but, on the other side, also cheats when he can, betrays the rights of men, or otherwise violates them. But although it is

possible that a universal law of nature might exist
in accordance with that maxim, it is impossible to
will that such a principle should have the universal
validity of a law of nature. For a will which resolved this would contradict itself, inasmuch as
many cases might occur in which one would have
need of the love and sympathy of others, and in
which, by such a law of nature, sprung from his
own will, he would deprive himself of all hope of
the aid he desires.

These are a few of the many actual duties, or at least what
we regard as such, which obviously fall into two classes on
the one principle that we have laid down. We must be able
to will that a maxim of our action should be a universal law.
This is the canon of the moral appreciation of the action
generally. Some actions are of such a character that their
maxim cannot without contradiction be even conceived as a
universal law of nature, far from it being possible that we
should will that it should be so. In others this intrinsic im-
possibility is not found, but still it is impossible to will that
their maxim should be raised to the universality of a law
of nature, since such a will would contradict itself. It is easily
seen that the former violate strict or rigorous (inflexible) duty;
the latter only laxer (meritorious) duty. Thus it has been
completely shown how all duties depend as regards the nature
of the obligation (not the object of the action) on the same
principle.

If now we attend to ourselves on occasion of any transgression of duty, we shall find that we in fact do not will that
our maxim should be a universal law, for that is impossible
for us; on the contrary, we will that the opposite should remain
a universal law, only we assume the liberty of making an
exception in our own favor or (just for this time only) in favor
of our inclination. Consequently if we considered all cases
from one and the same point of view, namely, that of reason,

we should find a contradiction in our own will, namely, that a certain principle should be objectively necessary as a universal law, and yet subjectively should not be universal, but admit of exceptions. As however we at one moment regard our action from the point of view of a will wholly conformed to reason, and then again look at the same action from the point of view of a will affected by inclination, there is not really any contradiction, but an antagonism of inclination to the precept of reason, whereby the universality of the principle is changed into a mere generality, so that the practical principle of reason shall meet the maxim half way. Now, although this cannot be justified in our own impartial judgement, yet it proves that we do really recognize the validity of the categorical imperative and (with all respect for it) only allow ourselves a few exceptions, which we think unimportant and forced from us.

We have thus established at least this much, that if duty is a conception which is to have any import and real legislative authority for our actions, it can only be expressed in categorical and not at all in hypothetical imperatives. We have also, which is of great importance, exhibited clearly and definitely for every practical application the content of the categorical imperative, which must contain the principle of all duty if there is such a thing at all. We have not yet, however, advanced so far as to prove *a priori* that there actually is such an imperative, that there is a practical law which commands absolutely of itself and without any other impulse, and that the following of this law is duty.

With the view of attaining to this, it is of extreme importance to remember that we must not allow ourselves to think of deducing the reality of this principle from the particular attributes of human nature. For duty is to be a practical, unconditional necessity of action; it must therefore hold for all rational beings (to whom an imperative can apply at all), and for this reason only be also a law for all human wills. On the contrary, whatever is deduced from the particular natural characteristics of humanity, from certain feelings and propensions, nay, even, if possible, from any particular tendency proper to human reason, and which need not necessarily hold for the will of every rational being; this may indeed supply us with a maxim, but not with a law; with a subjective principle on which we may have a propension and inclination to act, but not with an objective principle on which we should be enjoined to act, even though all our propensions, inclinations, and natural dispositions were opposed to it. In fact, the sublimity and intrinsic dignity of the command in duty are so much the more evident, the less the subjective impulses favor it and the more they oppose it, without being able in the slightest degree to weaken the obligation of the law or to diminish its validity.

Here then we see philosophy brought to a critical position, since it has to be firmly fixed, notwithstanding that it has nothing to support it in heaven or earth. Here it must show its purity as absolute director of its own laws, not the herald of those which are whispered to it by an implanted sense or who knows what tutelary nature. Although these may be better than nothing, yet they can never afford principles dictated by reason, which must have their source wholly *a priori* and thence their commanding authority, expecting everything from the supremacy of the law and the due respect for it, nothing from inclination, or else condemning the man to self-contempt and inward abhorrence.

Thus every empirical element is not only quite incapable of being an aid to the principle of morality, but is even highly prejudicial to the purity of morals, for the proper and inestimable worth of an absolutely good will consists just in this, that the principle of action is free from all influence of contingent grounds, which alone experience can furnish. We cannot too much or too often repeat our warning against this lax and even mean habit of thought which seeks for its principle amongst empirical motives and laws; for human reason in its weariness is glad to rest on this pillow, and in a dream of sweet illusions (in which, instead of Juno, it embraces a cloud) it substitutes for morality a bastard patched up from limbs of various derivation, which looks like anything one chooses to see in it, only not like virtue to one who has once beheld her in her true form.[10]

The question then is this: "Is it a necessary law for all rational beings that they should always judge of their actions by maxims of which they can themselves will that they should serve as universal laws?" If it is so, then it must be connected (altogether *a priori*) with the very conception of the will of a rational being generally. But in order to discover this connection we must, however reluctantly, take a step into metaphysic, although into a domain of it which is distinct from speculative philosophy, namely, the metaphysic of morals. In a practical philosophy, where it is not the reasons of what happens that we have to ascertain, but the laws of what ought to happen, even although it never does, i.e., objective practical laws, there it is not necessary to inquire into the reasons why anything pleases or displeases, how the pleasure of mere sensation differs from taste, and whether the latter is distinct from a general satisfaction of reason; on what the feeling of pleasure or pain rests, and how from it desires and inclinations arise, and from these again maxims by the co-operation of reason: for all this belongs to an empirical psychology, which would constitute the second part of physics, if we regard physics as the philosophy of nature, so far as it is based on empirical laws. But here we are concerned with objective practical laws and, consequently, with the relation of the will to itself so far as it is determined by reason alone, in which case whatever has reference to anything empirical is necessarily excluded; since if reason of itself alone determines the conduct (and it is the possibility of this that we are now investigating), it must necessarily do so *a priori*.

The will is conceived as a faculty of determining oneself to action in accordance with the conception of certain laws. And such a faculty can be found only in rational beings. Now that which serves the will as the objective ground of its self-determination is the end, and, if this is assigned by reason alone, it must hold for all rational beings. On the other hand, that which merely contains the ground of possibility of the action of which the effect is the end, this is called the means. The subjective ground of the desire is the spring, the objective ground of the volition is the motive; hence the distinction between subjective ends which rest on springs, and objective ends which depend on motives valid for every rational being. Practical principles are formal when they abstract from all subjective ends; they are material when they assume these, and therefore particular springs of action. The ends which a rational being proposes to himself at pleasure as effects of his actions (material ends) are all only relative, for it is only their relation to the particular desires of the subject that gives them their worth, which therefore cannot furnish principles universal and necessary for all rational beings and for every volition, that is to say practical laws. Hence all these relative ends can give rise only to hypothetical imperatives.

Supposing, however, that there were something whose existence has in itself an absolute worth, something which, being an end in itself, could be a source of definite laws; then in this and this alone would lie the source of a possible categorical imperative, i.e., a practical law.

Now I say: man and generally any rational being exists as an end in himself, not merely as a means to be arbitrarily used by this or that will, but in all his actions, whether they concern himself or other rational beings, must be always regarded at the same time as an end. All objects of the inclinations have only a conditional worth, for if the inclinations and the wants founded on them did not exist, then their object would be without value. But the inclinations, themselves being sources of want, are so far from having an absolute worth for which they should be desired that on the contrary it must be the universal wish of every rational being to be wholly free from them. Thus the worth of any object which is to be acquired by our action is always conditional. Beings whose existence depends not on our will but on nature's, have nevertheless, if they are irrational beings, only a relative value as means, and are therefore called things; rational beings, on the contrary, are called persons, because their very nature points them out as ends in themselves, that is as something which must not be used merely as means, and so far therefore restricts freedom of action (and is an object of respect). These, therefore, are not merely subjective ends whose existence has a worth for us as an effect of our action, but objective ends, that is, things whose existence is an end in itself; an end moreover for which no other can be substituted, which they should subserve merely as means, for otherwise nothing whatever would possess absolute worth; but if all worth were conditioned and therefore contingent, then there would be no supreme practical principle of reason whatever.

If then there is a supreme practical principle or, in respect of the human will, a categorical imperative, it must be one which, being drawn from the conception of that which is necessarily an end for everyone because it is an end in itself, constitutes an objective principle of will, and can therefore serve as a universal practical law. The foundation of this principle is: rational nature exists as an end in itself. Man necessarily conceives his own existence as being so; so far then this is a subjective principle of human actions. But every other rational being regards its existence similarly, just on the same rational principle that holds for me:[11] so that it is at the same time an objective principle, from which as a supreme practical law all laws of the will must be capable of being deduced. Accordingly the practical imperative will be as follows: So act as to treat humanity, whether in thine own person or in that of any other, in every case as an end withal, never as means only. We will now inquire whether this can be practically carried out.

To abide by the previous examples:

Firstly, under the head of necessary duty to oneself: He who contemplates suicide should ask himself whether his action can be consistent with the idea of humanity as an end in itself. If he destroys himself in order to escape from painful circumstances, he uses a person merely as a mean to maintain a tolerable condition up to the end of life. But a man is not a thing, that is to say, something which can be used merely as means, but must in all his actions be always considered as an end in himself. I cannot, therefore, dispose in any way of a man in my own person so as to mutilate him, to damage or kill him. (It belongs to ethics proper to define this principle more precisely, so as to avoid all misunderstanding, e.g., as to the amputation of the limbs in order to preserve myself, as to exposing my life to danger with a view to preserve it, etc. This question is therefore omitted here.)

Secondly, as regards necessary duties, or those of strict obligation, towards others: He who is thinking of making a lying promise to others will see at once that he would be using another man merely as a mean, without the latter containing at the same time the end in himself. For he whom I propose by such a promise to use for my own purposes cannot possibly assent to my mode of acting towards him and, therefore, cannot himself contain the end of this action. This violation of the principle of humanity in other men is more obvious if we take in examples of attacks on the freedom and property of others. For then it is clear that he who transgresses the rights of men intends to use the person of others merely as a means, without considering that as rational beings they ought always to be esteemed also as ends, that is, as beings who must be capable of containing in themselves the end of the very same action.[12]

Thirdly, as regards contingent (meritorious) duties to oneself: It is not enough that the action does not violate humanity in our own person as an end in itself, it must also harmonize with it. Now there are in humanity capacities of greater perfection, which belong to the end that nature has in view in regard to humanity in ourselves as the subject: to neglect these might perhaps be consistent with the maintenance of humanity as an end in itself, but not with the advancement of this end.

Fourthly, as regards meritorious duties towards others: The natural end which all men have is their own happiness. Now humanity might indeed subsist, although no one should contribute anything to the happiness of others, provided he did not intentionally withdraw anything from it; but after all this would only harmonize negatively not positively with humanity as an end in itself, if every one does not also endeavor, as far as in him lies, to forward the ends of others. For the ends of any subject which is an end in himself ought as far as possible to be my ends also, if that conception is to have its full effect with me.

This principle, that humanity and generally every rational nature is an end in itself (which is the supreme limiting condition of every man's freedom of action), is not borrowed from experience, firstly, because it is universal, applying as it does to all rational beings whatever, and experience is not capable of determining anything about them; secondly, because it does not present humanity as an end to men (subjectively), that is as an object which men do of themselves actually adopt as an end; but as an objective end, which must as a law constitute the supreme limiting condition of all our subjective ends, let them be what we will; it must therefore spring from pure reason. In fact the objective principle of all practical legislation lies (according to the first principle) in the rule and its form of universality which makes it capable of being a law (say, e.g., a law of nature); but the subjective principle is in the end; now by the second principle the subject of all ends is each rational being, inasmuch as it is an end in itself. Hence follows the third practical principle of the will, which is the ultimate condition of its harmony with universal practical reason, viz.: the idea of the will of every rational being as a universally legislative will.

On this principle all maxims are rejected which are inconsistent with the will being itself universal legislator. Thus the will is not subject simply to the law, but so subject that it must be regarded as itself giving the law and, on this ground only, subject to the law (of which it can regard itself as the author).

In the previous imperatives, namely, that based on the conception of the conformity of actions to general laws, as in a physical system of nature, and that based on the universal prerogative of rational beings as ends in themselves—these imperatives, just because they were conceived as categorical, excluded from any share in their authority all admixture of any interest as a spring of action; they were, however, only assumed to be categorical, because such an assumption was necessary to explain the conception of duty. But we could not prove independently that there are practical propositions which command categorically, nor can it be proved in this section; one thing, however, could be done, namely, to indicate in the imperative itself, by some determinate expression, that in the case of volition from duty all interest is renounced, which is the specific criterion of categorical as distinguished from hypothetical imperatives. This is done in the present (third) formula of the principle, namely, in the idea of the will of every rational being as a universally legislating will.

For although a will which is subject to laws may be attached to this law by means of an interest, yet a will which is itself a supreme lawgiver so far as it is such cannot possibly depend on any interest, since a will so dependent would itself still need another law restricting the interest of its self-love by the condition that it should be valid as universal law.

Thus the principle that every human will is a will which in all its maxims gives universal laws,[13] provided it be otherwise justified, would be very well adapted to be the categorical imperative, in this respect, namely, that just because of the idea of universal legislation it is not based on interest, and therefore it alone among all possible imperatives can be unconditional. Or still better, converting the proposition, if there is a categorical imperative (i.e., a law for the will of every rational being), it can only command that everything be done from maxims of one's will regarded as a will which could at the same time will that it should itself give universal laws, for in that case only the practical principle and the imperative which it obeys are unconditional, since they cannot be based on any interest.

Looking back now on all previous attempts to discover the principle of morality, we need not wonder why they all failed. It was seen that man was bound to laws by duty, but it was not observed that the laws to which he is subject are only those of his own giving, though at the same time they are universal, and that he is only bound to act in conformity with his own will; a will, however, which is designed by nature to give universal laws. For when one has conceived man only as subject to a law (no matter what), then this law required some interest, either by way of attraction or constraint, since it did not originate as a law from his own will, but this will was according to a law obliged by something else to act in a certain manner. Now by this necessary consequence all the labor spent in finding a supreme principle of duty was irrevocably lost. For men never elicited duty, but only a necessity of acting from a certain interest. Whether this interest was private or otherwise, in any case the imperative must be conditional and could not by any means be capable of being a moral command. I will therefore call this the principle of autonomy of the will, in contrast with every other which I accordingly reckon as heteronomy.

The conception of the will of every rational being as one which must consider itself as giving in all the maxims of its will universal laws, so as to judge itself and its actions from this point of view, this conception leads to another which depends on it and is very fruitful, namely that of a kingdom of ends.

By a kingdom I understand the union of different rational beings in a system by common laws. Now since it is by laws that ends are determined as regards their universal validity, hence, if we abstract from the personal differences of rational beings and likewise from all the content of their private ends, we shall be able to conceive all ends combined in a systematic whole (including both rational beings as ends in themselves, and also the special ends which each may propose to himself), that is to say, we can conceive a kingdom of ends, which on the preceding principles is possible.

For all rational beings come under the law that each of them must treat itself and all others never merely as means, but in every case at the same time as ends in themselves. Hence results a systematic union of rational being by common objective laws, i.e., a kingdom which may be called a kingdom of ends, since what these laws have in view is just the relation of these beings to one another as ends and means. It is certainly only an ideal.

A rational being belongs as a member to the kingdom of ends when, although giving universal laws in it, he is also himself subject to these laws. He belongs to it as sovereign when, while giving laws, he is not subject to the will of any other.

A rational being must always regard himself as giving laws either as member or as sovereign in a kingdom of ends which is rendered possible by the freedom of will. He cannot, however, maintain the latter position merely by the maxims of his will, but only in case he is a completely independent being without wants and with unrestricted power adequate to his will.

Morality consists then in the reference of all action to the legislation which alone can render a kingdom of ends possible. This legislation must be capable of existing in every rational being and of emanating from his will, so that the principle of this will is never to act on any maxim which could not without contradiction be also a universal law and, accordingly, always so to act that the will could at the same time regard itself as giving in its maxims universal laws. If now the maxims of rational beings are not by their own nature coincident with this objective principle, then the necessity of acting on it is called practical necessitation, i.e., duty. Duty does not apply to the sovereign in the kingdom of ends, but it does to every member of it and to all in the same degree.

The practical necessity of acting on this principle, i.e., duty, does not rest at all on feelings, impulses, or inclinations, but solely on the relation of rational beings to one another, a relation in which the will of a rational being must always be regarded as legislative, since otherwise it could not be conceived as an end in itself. Reason then refers every maxim of the will, regarding it as legislating universally, to every other will and also to every action towards oneself; and this not on account of any other practical motive or any future advantage, but from the idea of the dignity of a rational being, obeying no law but that which he himself also gives.

In the kingdom of ends everything has either value or dignity. Whatever has a value can be replaced by something else which is equivalent; whatever, on the other hand, is above all value, and therefore admits of no equivalent, has a dignity.

Whatever has reference to the general inclinations and wants of mankind has a market value; whatever, without presupposing a want, corresponds to a certain taste, that is to a satisfaction in the mere purposeless play of our faculties, has a fancy value; but that which constitutes the condition under which alone anything can be an end in itself, this has not merely a relative worth, i.e., value, but an intrinsic worth, that is, dignity.

Now morality is the condition under which alone a rational being can be an end in himself, since by this alone it is possible that he should be a legislating member in the kingdom of ends. Thus morality, and humanity as capable of it, is that which alone has dignity. Skill and diligence in labor have a market value; wit, lively imagination, and humor, have fancy value; on the other hand, fidelity to promises, benevolence from principle (not from instinct), have an intrinsic worth. Neither nature nor art contains anything which in default of these it could put in their place, for their worth consists not in the effects which spring from them, not in the use and advantage which they secure, but in the disposition of mind, that is, the maxims of the will which are ready to manifest themselves in such actions, even though they should not have the desired effect. These actions also need no recommendation from any subjective taste or sentiment, that they may be looked on with immediate favor and satisfaction: they need no immediate propension or feeling for them; they exhibit the will that performs them as an object of an immediate respect, and nothing but reason is required to impose them on the will; not to flatter it into them, which, in the case of duties, would be a contradiction. This estimation therefore shows that the worth of such a disposition is dignity, and places it infinitely above all value, with which it cannot for a moment be brought into comparison or competition without as it were violating its sanctity.

What then is it which justifies virtue or the morally good disposition, in making such lofty claims? It is nothing less than the privilege it secures to the rational being of participating in the giving of universal laws, by which it qualifies him to be a member of a possible kingdom of ends, a privilege to which he was already destined by his own nature as being an end in himself and, on that account, legislating in the kingdom of ends; free as regards all laws of physical nature, and obeying those only which he himself gives, and by which his maxims can belong to a system of universal law, to which at the same time he submits himself. For nothing has any worth except what the law assigns it. Now the legislation itself which assigns the worth of everything must for that very reason possess dignity, that is, an unconditional incomparable

worth; and the word respect alone supplies a becoming expression for the esteem which a rational being must have for
it. Autonomy then is the basis of the dignity of human and
of every rational nature.

The three modes of presenting the principle of morality
that have been adduced are at bottom only so many formulae
of the very same law, and each of itself involves the other
two. There is, however, a difference in them, but it is rather
subjectively than objectively practical, intended namely to
bring an idea of the reason nearer to intuition (by means of
a certain analogy) and thereby nearer to feeling. All maxims,
in fact, have:

1. A form, consisting in universality; and in this view
   the formula of the moral imperative is expressed
   thus, that the maxims must be so chosen as if they
   were to serve as universal laws of nature.
2. A matter, namely, an end, and here the formula
   says that the rational being, as it is an end by its
   own nature and therefore an end in itself, must in
   every maxim serve as the condition limiting all
   merely relative and arbitrary ends.
3. A complete characterization of all maxims by
   means of that formula, namely, that all maxims
   ought by their own legislation to harmonize with
   a possible kingdom of ends as with a kingdom of
   nature.[14] There is a progress here in the order of
   the categories of unity of the form of the will (its
   universality), plurality of the matter (the objects,
   i.e., the ends), and totality of the system of these. In
   forming our moral judgement of actions, it is better
   to proceed always on the strict method and start
   from the general formula of the categorical imperative: Act according to a maxim which can at the
   same time make itself a universal law. If, however,
   we wish to gain an entrance for the moral law, it is

very useful to bring one and the same action under
the three specified conceptions, and thereby as far
as possible to bring it nearer to intuition.

We can now end where we started at the beginning, namely,
with the conception of a will unconditionally good. That will
is absolutely good which cannot be evil—in other words,
whose maxim, if made a universal law, could never contradict
itself. This principle, then, is its supreme law: "Act always on
such a maxim as thou canst at the same time will to be a
universal law"; this is the sole condition under which a will
can never contradict itself; and such an imperative is categorical. Since the validity of the will as a universal law for possible
actions is analogous to the universal connection of the existence of things by general laws, which is the formal notion
of nature in general, the categorical imperative can also be
expressed thus: Act on maxims which can at the same time
have for their object themselves as universal laws of nature.
Such then is the formula of an absolutely good will.

Rational nature is distinguished from the rest of nature by
this, that it sets before itself an end. This end would be the
matter of every good will. But since in the idea of a will that
is absolutely good without being limited by any condition (of
attaining this or that end) we must abstract wholly from every
end to be effected (since this would make every will only
relatively good), it follows that in this case the end must be
conceived, not as an end to be effected, but as an independently
existing end. Consequently it is conceived only negatively, i.e.,
as that which we must never act against and which, therefore,
must never be regarded merely as means, but must in every
volition be esteemed as an end likewise. Now this end can be
nothing but the subject of all possible ends, since this is also
the subject of a possible absolutely good will; for such a will
cannot without contradiction be postponed to any other
object. The principle: "So act in regard to every rational
being (thyself and others), that he may always have a place

in thy maxim as an end in himself," is accordingly essentially identical with this other: "Act upon a maxim which, at the same time, involves its own universal validity for every rational being." For that in using means for every end I should limit my maxim by the condition of its holding good as a law for every subject, this comes to the same thing as that the fundamental principle of all maxims of action must be that the subject of all ends, i.e., the rational being himself, be never employed merely as means, but as the supreme condition restricting the use of all means, that is, in every case as an end likewise.

It follows incontestably that, to whatever laws any rational being may be subject, he being an end in himself must be able to regard himself as also legislating universally in respect of these same laws, since it is just this fitness of his maxims for universal legislation that distinguishes him as an end in himself; also it follows that this implies his dignity (prerogative) above all mere physical beings, that he must always take his maxims from the point of view which regards himself and, likewise, every other rational being as law-giving beings (on which account they are called persons). In this way a world of rational beings (*mundus intelligibilis*) is possible as a kingdom of ends, and this by virtue of the legislation proper to all persons as members. Therefore every rational being must so act as if he were by his maxims in every case a legislating member in the universal kingdom of ends. The formal principle of these maxims is: "So act as if thy maxim were to serve likewise as the universal law (of all rational beings)." A kingdom of ends is thus only possible on the analogy of a kingdom of nature, the former however only by maxims, that is, self-imposed rules, the latter only by the laws of efficient causes acting under necessitation from without. Nevertheless, although the system of nature is looked upon as a machine, yet so far as it has reference to rational beings as its ends, it is given on this account the name of a kingdom of nature. Now such a kingdom of ends would be actually realized by means of maxims conforming to the canon which the categorical imperative prescribes to all rational beings, if they were universally followed. But although a rational being, even if he punctually follows this maxim himself, cannot reckon upon all others being therefore true to the same, nor expect that the kingdom of nature and its orderly arrangements shall be in harmony with him as a fitting member, so as to form a kingdom of ends to which he himself contributes, that is to say, that it shall favor his expectation of happiness, still that law: "Act according to the maxims of a member of a merely possible kingdom of ends legislating in it universally," remains in its full force, inasmuch as it commands categorically. And it is just in this that the paradox lies; that the mere dignity of man as a rational creature, without any other end or advantage to be attained thereby, in other words, respect for a mere idea, should yet serve as an inflexible precept of the will, and that it is precisely in this independence of the maxim on all such springs of action that its sublimity consists; and it is this that makes every rational subject worthy to be a legislative member in the kingdom of ends: for otherwise he would have to be conceived only as subject to the physical law of his wants. And although we should suppose the kingdom of nature and the kingdom of ends to be united under one sovereign, so that the latter kingdom thereby ceased to be a mere idea and acquired true reality, then it would no doubt gain the accession of a strong spring, but by no means any increase of its intrinsic worth. For this sole absolute lawgiver must, notwithstanding this, be always conceived as estimating the worth of rational beings only by their disinterested behavior, as prescribed to themselves from that idea [the dignity of man] alone. The essence of things is not altered by their external relations, and that which, abstracting from these, alone constitutes the absolute worth of man, is also that by which he must be judged, whoever the judge may be, and even by the Supreme Being. Morality, then, is the relation of actions to the relation of actions will, that is, to the autonomy of potential universal legislation by its maxims. An action that is consistent with the autonomy of the will is permitted; one that does not agree therewith is forbidden. A will whose maxims necessarily coincide with the laws of autonomy is a holy will, good absolutely. The dependence of a will not absolutely good on the principle of autonomy (moral necessitation) is obligation. This, then, cannot be applied to a holy being. The objective necessity of actions from obligation is called duty.

From what has just been said, it is easy to see how it happens that, although the conception of duty implies subjection to the law, we yet ascribe a certain dignity and sublimity to the person who fulfills all his duties. There is not, indeed, any sublimity in him, so far as he is subject to the moral law; but inasmuch as in regard to that very law he is likewise a legislator, and on that account alone subject to it, he has sublimity. We have also shown above that neither fear nor inclination, but simply respect for the law, is the spring which can give actions a moral worth. Our own will, so far as we suppose it to act only under the condition that its maxims are potentially universal laws, this ideal will which is possible to us is the proper object of respect; and the dignity of humanity consists just in this capacity of being universally legislative, though with the condition that it is itself subject to this same legislation.

Notes

1. A maxim is the subjective principle of volition. The objective principle (i.e., that which would also serve subjectively as a practical principle to all rational beings if reason had full power over the faculty of desire) is the practical law.

2. It might be here objected to me that I take refuge behind the word respect in an obscure feeling, instead of giving a distinct solution of the question by a concept of the reason. But although respect is a feeling, it is not a feeling received through influence, but is self-wrought by a rational concept, and, therefore, is specifically distinct from all feelings of the former kind, which

may be referred either to inclination or fear. What I recognize
immediately as a law for me, I recognize with respect. This
merely signifies the consciousness that my will is subordinate to
a law, without the intervention of other influences on my sense.
The immediate determination of the will by the law and the
consciousness of this, is called respect, so that this is regarded as
an effect of the law on the subject, and not as the cause of it.
Respect is properly the conception of a worth which thwarts my
self-love. Accordingly it is something which is considered neither
as an object of inclination nor of fear, although it has something
analogous to both. The object of respect is the law only, and
that the law which we impose on ourselves and yet recognize
as necessary in itself. As a law, we are subjected to it without
consulting self-love; as imposed by us on ourselves, it is a result
of our will. In the former aspect it has an analogy to fear, in the
latter to inclination. Respect for a person is properly only respect
for the law (of honesty, etc.) of which he gives us an example.
Since we also look on the improvement of our talents as a duty,
we consider that we see in a person of talents, as it were, the
example of a law (viz., to become like him in this by exercise),
and this constitutes our respect. All so-called moral interest
consists simply in respect for the law.

  3. I have a letter from the late excellent Sulzer, in which he
asks me what can be the reason that moral instruction,
although containing much that is convincing for the reason, yet
accomplishes so little? My answer was postponed in order that I
might make it complete. But it is simply this: that the teachers
themselves have not got their own notions clear, and when they
endeavor to make up for this by raking up motives of moral
goodness from every quarter, trying to make their physic right
strong, they spoil it. For the commonest understanding shows
that if we imagine, on the one hand, an act of honesty done with
steadfast mind, apart from every view to advantage of any kind
in this world or another, and even under the greatest temptations
of necessity or allurement, and, on the other hand, a similar act
which was affected, in however low a degree, by a foreign
motive, the former leaves far behind and eclipses the second; it
elevates the soul and inspires the wish to be able to act in like
manner oneself. Even moderately young children feel this

impression, and one should never represent duties to them in any other light.

4. The dependence of the desires on sensations is called inclination, and this accordingly always indicates a want. The dependence of a contingently determinable will on principles of reason is called an interest. This therefore is found only in the case of a dependent will which does not always of itself conform to reason; in the Divine will we cannot conceive any interest. But the human will can also take an interest in a thing without therefore acting from interest. The former signifies the practical interest in the action, the latter the pathological in the object of the action. The former indicates only dependence of the will on principles of reason in themselves; the second, dependence on principles of reason for the sake of inclination, reason supplying only the practical rules of how the requirement of the inclination may be satisfied. In the first case the action interests me; in the second the object of the action (because it is pleasant to me). We have seen in the first section that in an action done from duty we must look not to the interest in the object, but only to that in the action itself, and in its rational principle (viz., the law).

5. The word prudence is taken in two senses: in the one it may bear the name of knowledge of the world, in the other that of private prudence. The former is a man's ability to influence others so as to use them for his own purposes. The latter is the sagacity to combine all these purposes for his own lasting benefit. This latter is properly that to which the value even of the former is reduced, and when a man is prudent in the former sense, but not in the latter, we might better say of him that he is clever and cunning, but, on the whole, imprudent.

6. It seems to me that the proper signification of the word pragmatic may be most accurately defined in this way. For sanctions are called pragmatic which flow properly not from the law of the states as necessary enactments, but from precaution for the general welfare. A history is composed pragmatically when it teaches prudence, i.e., instructs the world how it can provide for its interests better than or at least as well as, the men of former time.

7. I connect the act with the will without presupposing any condition resulting from any inclination, but *a priori*, and therefore

necessarily (though only objectively, i.e., assuming the idea of a
reason possessing full power over all subjective motives). This is
accordingly a practical proposition which does not deduce the
willing of an action by mere analysis from another already
presupposed (for we have not such a perfect will), but connects it
immediately with the conception of the will of a rational being, as
something not contained in it.

8. A maxim is a subjective principle of action, and must be
distinguished from the objective principle, namely, practical law.
The former contains the practical rule set by reason according to
the conditions of the subject (often its ignorance or its inclinations),
so that it is the principle on which the subject acts; but the law is
the objective principle valid for every rational being, and is the
principle on which it ought to act that is an imperative.

9. It must be noted here that I reserve the division of duties for
a future metaphysic of morals; so that I give it here only as an
arbitrary one (in order to arrange my examples). For the rest, I
understand by a perfect duty one that admits no exception in
favor of inclination and then I have not merely external but also
internal perfect duties. This is contrary to the use of the word
adopted in the schools; but I do not intend to justify there, as it is
all one for my purpose whether it is admitted or not.

10. To behold virtue in her proper form is nothing else but to
contemplate morality stripped of all admixture of sensible things
and of every spurious ornament of reward or self-love. How
much she then eclipses everything else that appears charming to
the affections, every one may readily perceive with the least
exertion of his reason, if it be not wholly spoiled for abstraction.

11. This proposition is here stated as a postulate. The ground
of it will be found in the concluding section.

12. Let it not be thought that the common "quod tibi non vis
fieri, etc." could serve here as the rule or principle. For it is only a
deduction from the former, though with several limitations; it
cannot be a universal law, for it does not contain the principle of
duties to oneself, nor of the duties of benevolence to others (for
many a one would gladly consent that others should not benefit
him, provided only that he might be excused from showing
benevolence to them), nor finally that of duties of strict obligation

to one another, for on this principle the criminal might argue against the judge who punishes him, and so on.

13. I may be excused from adducing examples to elucidate this principle, as those which have already been used to elucidate the categorical imperative and its formula would all serve for the like purpose here.

14. Teleology considers nature as a kingdom of ends; ethics regards a possible kingdom of ends as a kingdom nature. In the first case, the kingdom of ends is a theoretical idea, adopted to explain what actually is. In the latter it is a practical idea, adopted to bring about that which is not yet, but which can be realized by our conduct, namely, if it conforms to this idea.

[Paul Tillich, "The Religious Dimension of the Moral Imperative," in *Morality and Beyond* (New York: Harper & Row, 1976), 17–30.]

I

The Religious Dimension of the Moral Imperative

In the first three chapters of this book, the immanence of the religious in the moral shall be considered from three directions. The first chapter deals with the religious *dimension* of the moral imperative, the second with the religious *source* of the moral demands, and the third with the religious *element* in moral motivation.

To understand the meaning of the phrase "moral imperative," we must distinguish the three basic functions of the human spirit: morality, culture, and religion. When we call them functions of man's "spirit," we point to the dynamic unity of body and mind, of vitality and rationality, of the conscious and the unconscious, of the emotional and the intellectual. In every function of the human spirit the whole person is involved, and not merely one part or one element. As I have often insisted, we must revive the term "spirit" as designating a natural quality of man. It cannot be replaced by "mind" because "mind" is overweighted by its intellectual aspect.

None of the three functions of the spirit ever appears in isolation from the other two. They must be distinguished, nonetheless, because they are able to relate to one another in many different ways. Most concisely, we might say: Morality is the constitution of the bearer of the spirit, the centered person; culture points to the creativity of the spirit and also to the totality of its creations; and religion is the self-transcendence of the spirit toward what is ultimate and unconditioned in being and meaning.

The first of these functions is our direct and primary subject. But in order to deal with it adequately we must continually refer to the other two. This presents a difficulty hardly to be resolved in an essay such as this, and overcome only within a system that comprises the whole of man's interpretation of himself and the meaning of his life (which I undertook to develop in my *Systematic Theology*). The present study must presuppose but cannot develop such an interpretation; however, we must refer to it, and derive from it a possible solution to the problem at hand—"the religious principles of moral action."

The moral act establishes man as a person, and as a bearer of the spirit. It is the unconditional character of the moral imperative that gives ultimate seriousness to both culture and to religion. Without it, culture would deteriorate into an aesthetic or utilitarian enterprise, and religion into an emotional distortion of mysticism. It was the prophetic message, as recorded in the Old Testament, that contrasted the moral imperative, in terms of the demand for justice, with both the culture and the religion of its time. The message is one of ultimate seriousness and has no equivalent in any other religion. The seriousness of Christianity depends upon it, as does also any ultimate seriousness in Western culture. Science and the arts, politics, education—all become empty and self-destructive if, in their creation, the moral imperative is disregarded. The imperative exhibits itself in scientific and artistic honesty to the extent of self-sacrifice; in one's commitment to humanity and justice in social relations and political actions; and in the love of one toward the other, as a consequence of experiencing the divine love. These are examples which demonstrate that, without the immanence of the moral imperative, both culture and religion disintegrate because of a lack of ultimate seriousness.

The moral imperative is the command to become what one potentially is, a *person* within a community of persons. Only man, in the limit of our experience, can become a person, because only man is a completely centered self, having himself as a self in the face of a world to which he belongs and from which he is, at the same time, separated. This dual relation to his world, belongingness and separation, makes it possible for him to ask questions and find answers, to receive and make demands. As a centered self and individual, man can respond in knowledge and action to the stimuli that reach him from the world to which he belongs; but because he also *confronts* his world, and in this sense is free from it, he can respond "responsibly," namely, after deliberation and decision rather than through a determined compulsion. This is his greatness, but also his danger: It enables him to act *against* the moral demand. He can surrender to the disintegrating forces that tend to control the personal center and to destroy its unity. But before we pursue this line of thought, we must consider more thoroughly some of our concepts up to this point.

Man has a world, namely, a structured whole of innumerable parts, a *cosmos*, as the Greeks called it, because of its structured character, which makes it accessible to man through acts of creative receiving and transforming. Having a world is more than having environment. Of course, man, like any other being, has environment; but in contrast to the higher animals, for example, he is not bound to it. He can transcend it in any direction, in imagination, thought, and action (e.g., social utopias or ontological concepts or space exploration). Man has "world" through every part of his environment. His encounter with any of the objects surrounding him is always an encounter with the universe manifest in a particular object. Man never encounters *this* tree only as *this* tree, but also as *tree*, one of many trees, as an example of the species tree (in itself a special manifestation of the universal power of being).

Such an encounter presupposes freedom from the particular and the ability to see the universal within the particular. The manifestation of this freedom is language. Language lives in universals. It is one and the same thing to have world, to transcend environment, and to speak in concepts and meaningful propositions. All this constitutes man's essential freedom and is the presupposition of man's experience of the moral imperative.

The moral imperative is the demand to become actually what one is essentially and therefore potentially. It is the power of man's being, given to him by nature, which he shall actualize in time and space. His true being shall become his actual being—this is the moral imperative. And since his true being is the being of a person in a community of persons, the moral imperative has this content: to become a person. Every moral act is an act in which an individual self establishes itself as a person.

Therefore, a moral act is not an act in obedience to an external law, human or divine. It is the inner law of our true being, of our essential or created nature, which demands that we actualize what follows from it. And an anti-moral act is not the transgression of one or several precisely circumscribed commands but an act that contradicts the self-realization of the person as a person and drives toward disintegration. It disrupts the centeredness of the person by giving predominance to partial trends, passions, desires, fears, and anxieties. The central control is weakened, often almost removed. And when this happens, and other partial trends also aspire to predominance, the self is split and the conflicting trends make it their battlefield. The "will," in the sense of a self that acts from the centered totality of its being, is enslaved. Freedom is replaced by compulsion. Deliberation and decision, the hallmarks of freedom, become mere façades for overwhelming drives that predetermine the decision. The voice of man's essential being is silenced, step by step; and his disintegrating self, his depersonalization, shows the nature of the anti-moral act and, by contrast, the nature of the moral act.

The moral act as the self-actualization of the centered self or the constitution of the person as a person has analogies in the realm of all living beings, including man from the biological point of view. The analogy to the diminution or loss of centeredness in man is the psychosomatic phenomenon of disease. In disease, some processes that are necessary elements in the whole of a life process take an independent course and endanger the functioning of the whole. The cancerous growth of parts of the body is the most illuminating analogy to what happens in the centered self when particular trends conquer the center and destroy the unity of balanced trends. The analogy between the anti-moral act and bodily disease is in many (somehow in all) cases more than an analogy. Both are expressions of the universal ambiguity of life, according to which the processes of self-integration are continually combated by movements toward disintegration. For the ethical problem this means that the moral act is always a victory over disintegrating forces and that its aim is the actualization of man as a centered and therefore free person.

At this point a short semantic remark seems necessary. In this study, I use the terms "morality," "morals," and "moral" throughout most of the text. And sometimes the term "ethical" appears. There would be no confusion if, as I now suggest, we defined ethics as the "science of the moral." But this is not a generally accepted definition, the chief reason being that the word "moral," through historical accidents, has received several distorting connotations. Since the eighteenth century, at least in Europe, it has carried the implication of "moralism" in the sense of graceless legalistic ethics. And in the United States, it has, under the influence of Puritanism, taken on a sexual signification: To be "amoral" means to be sexually lawless, or at least to deny conventional sex ethics. Because of these two connotations, one has tried to replace "moral" with "ethical." Were this generally accepted, however, the term "ethical" would soon acquire the connotation of "moral," and there would be no change. Therefore, I recommend that "ethical" be reserved for the *theory* of morals and that the term "moral" and its derivatives be purged of those associations and used to describe the moral act itself in its fundamental significance.

We have discussed the nature of the moral act, its all-permeating character, and its immanence in the other two chief functions of man's spirit—the cultural and the religious. We must now ask: What is the religious dimension of the moral imperative, and (in Chapter II) what is the relation of cultural creativity to morality?

In answer to the first question, we can say: The religious dimension of the moral imperative is its unconditional character. This, of course, leads to a subsequent question: Why is the moral imperative unconditional, and in which respects can one call it so and in which not? In our daily life we use innumerable imperatives, but most of them are conditional: "You ought to leave *now*, if you wish to catch your plane." But perhaps you prefer to stay, even though you miss the plane. This obviously is a conditional imperative. However, if getting to the plane should be a matter of life and death, as, for example, in the case of a physician who must immediately operate upon a patient, the conditional imperative becomes unconditional. To miss the plane through negligence would then be an anti-moral act and would affect the person of the physician in a disintegrating manner. We might compare the disintegrating effect that the failure to save a drowning woman has on the main character in Camus' *The Fall*.

There are many cases in which conditional imperatives have some bearing on an unconditional imperative. The missing of the plane might also arouse anxiety in those who expect the arrival of a friend. And there are cases in which several imperatives compete for supreme validity, and in which the decision is a moral risk. But despite these "mixed" cases, the moral imperative in itself is, as Immanuel Kant called it, "categorical" rather than "hypothetical," or as I would say, unconditional as opposed to conditional.

We may ask, however, whether a moral decision can stand under an unconditional imperative if the decision is a moral risk—the "risk" implying that it might prove to be the wrong decision. The answer to this question is that the unconditional character does not refer to the content but to the form of the moral decision. Whichever side of a moral alternative might be chosen, however great the risk in a bold decision may be, if it be a *moral* decision it is dependent on only the pure "ought to be" of the moral imperative. And should anyone be in doubt as to which of several possible acts conforms to the moral imperative, he should be reminded that each of them might be justified in a particular situation, but that whatever he chooses must be done with the consciousness of standing under an unconditional imperative. The doubt concerning the justice of a moral act does not contradict the certainty of its ultimate seriousness.

The assertion of the intrinsically religious character of the moral imperative can be criticized from different points of view. Theology can strongly affirm the unconditioned character of the moral imperative but deny that this character makes it religious. Moral commands, one argues then, are religious because they are divine commandments. They are ultimately serious because they express the "Will of God." This alone makes them unconditional. God could have willed differently, and we must open our eyes to His revelation in order to know what His Will actually is. Such an argument, of course, would exclude any kind of secular ethics. Not only the content but also the unconditional character of the moral imperative would have to be sanctioned by a divine command and conserved in holy traditions or sacred books.

I maintain, however, that the term "Will of God" can and must be understood differently. It is not an external will imposed upon us, an arbitrary law laid down by a heavenly tyrant, who is strange to our essential nature and therefore whom we resist justifiably from the point of view of our nature. The "Will of God" for us is precisely our essential being with all its potentialities, our created nature declared as "very good" by God, as, in terms of the Creation myth, He "saw everything that he made." For us the "Will of God" is manifest in our essential being, and only because of this can we accept the moral imperative as valid. It is not a strange law that demands our obedience but the "silent voice" of our own nature as man, and as man with an individual character.

But we must go one further step. We can say: To fulfill one's own nature is certainly a moral demand intrinsic to one's being. But why is it an unconditional imperative? Do I not have the right to leave my potentialities unfulfilled, to remain less than a person, to contradict my essential goodness, and thus to destroy myself? As a being that has the freedom of self-contradiction, I should have the right to this possibility, and to waste myself! The moral imperative is unconditional only if I choose to affirm my own essential nature, and *this is* a condition! The answer to this argument is the experience that has been expressed in the doctrine of the infinite value of every human soul in the view of the Eternal. It is not an external prohibition against self-destruction—bodily, psychologically, or morally—that we experience in states of despair but the silent voice of our own being which denies us the right to self-destruction. It is the awareness of our belonging to a dimension that transcends our own finite freedom and our ability to affirm or to negate ourselves. So I maintain my basic assertion that the unconditional character of the moral imperative is its religious quality. No religious heteronomy, subjection to external commands, is implied if we maintain the immanence of religion in the moral command.

The intrinsically religious character of the moral imperative is indirectly denied by the philosophy of values. Its representatives think in terms of a hierarchy of values in which the value of the holy may or may not find a place; when it does, it is often on the top of this pyramid, above the moral, legal, social, political, and economic values. For our problem, this means first of all that values lie above and below each other and that there can be no immanence of one within another. The value of the holy, for example, cannot be immanent in the value of the good, and conversely. The relationship is external and may lead to the elimination of one or the other—most frequently, in this case, the value of the holy.

A second character of the value theory has a considerable bearing on our problem. The establishment of values and their relationships presupposes a valuating subject, and the question arises: How can values that are relative to a valuating individual or group (e.g., pleasure values) be separated from values that are valid by their very nature regardless of personal or social attitudes? If there are such "absolute values" (absolute in the sense of being independent of a valuating subject), what is the source of their absoluteness, how can they be discovered, how are they related to reality, and what is their ontological standing? These questions lead unavoidably to a situation that the value theory by its very nature tries to avoid—namely, a doctrine of being, an ontology. For values have reality only if they are rooted in reality. Their validity is an expression of their ontological foundation. *Being precedes value*, but value fulfills being. Therefore, the value theory, in its search for absolute values, is thrown back upon the ontological question of the source of values in being.

A third way in which the religious dimension of the moral imperative is questioned can be described as the attempt, with the help of psychological and sociological explanations, to deny the unconditional character of the moral altogether. The psychological impact of realities like the demanding and threatening parents, or of doctrines like that of the commanding and punishing God, evokes the feeling of something unconditionally serious from which there is no escape and with which there can be no compromise.

The same argument can be strengthened by sociological considerations. For example, one can derive, like Nietzsche, the shaping of the conscience of the masses from centuries of pressure exercised by the ruling groups, who did not hesitate to employ all, even the most cruel, tools of suppression— military, legal, educational, psychological. From generation to generation, this pressure produced an increasing internalization of commands, namely, the sense of standing under an inner unconditional command, an absolute moral imperative.

This type of argument seems convincing. But it is circular because it presupposes what it tries to prove—the identity of two qualitatively different structures. In the one case, persons and groups are bound by traditions, conventions, and authorities, subjection to which is demanded by the conscience, which may be weak or strong, compromising or insistent, healthy or compulsory, reasonable or fanatic. Psychological or sociological explanations of such states of mind are fully justified. Nothing that happens in the mind should be exempt from psychological or sociological exploration and explanation. But within this structure of causation, another is manifest—what we might call the "structure of meaning" or, to use a famous medieval term revived by modern phenomenology, the structure of "intentionality" or the *noetic* structure (from *nous*, "mind"). This structure would be evident, for example, should a mathematician, psychologically and sociologically conditioned like everyone else, discover a new mathematical proposition. The validity of this proposition is independent of the series of conditions which made the discovery possible. In a similar way, the meaning of the unconditional in being and in what ought-to-be appears within the psychological and sociological processes which make its appearance possible. But its validity is not dependent on the structure in which it appears. Psychological and sociological pressures may provide occasion for the appearance of such structures, but they cannot produce the meaning of the unconditional. However strong the pressures be, they are themselves conditioned, and it is possible to contradict them and to be liberated from them, as, for example, from the father-image or from the socially produced conscience. This is not possible with regard to the unconditional character of the moral imperative. One can, of course, discard every particular content for the sake of another, but one cannot discard the moral imperative itself without the self-destruction of one's essential nature and one's eternal relationship. For these reasons, the attempts to undercut the unconditional character of the moral imperative by psychological and sociological arguments must fail.

There is, however, a more fundamental question, raised and thoroughly discussed by the ancient ethical philosophers, namely, the question of the moral aim. We have called it "becoming a person within a community of persons," and we have indicated that the centered person is the bearer of the spirit, its creativity, and its self-transcendence. Insofar as it is the moral aim to constitute and preserve the person with these potentialities, we can say that the moral imperative demands the actualization of man's created potentiality. But now the question arises: Is this an unconditional demand? The answer depends on the idea of man's intrinsic aim, of the *telos* for which he is created. If the aim implies something above finitude and transitoriness, the fulfillment of this aim is infinitely significant, or unconditional in its seriousness. When Plato said that the *telos* of man is "to become as much as possible similar to the God," such a *telos* gives unconditional character to the moral imperative. If, however, the *telos* is, as in the hedonistic school, the greatest possible amount of pleasure to be derived from life, no unconditional imperative is at work, but merely the very much-conditioned advice to calculate well what amount of pain must be suffered in order to attain the greatest possible amount of pleasure. Between these two extremes of the definition of man's inner *telos* are several definitions which set a finite aim according to the formulation, but in which something unconditional with respect to the moral imperative shines through. This is true of utilitarianism, in which the moral imperative demands work for "the greatest happiness of the greatest number." Here pleasure is replaced by "happiness," and above all, it is not the individual happiness, but that of the many, that is the aim. And the happiness of the many is not possible without self-restraint in the individual's search for happiness. Therefore, a demand appears that cannot be derived from the merely natural trends of the individual, a demand that implies the acceptance of the other person as a person, and an unconditional element besides, whether acknowledged or not.

The Epicureans deal with the problems of the *telos* and the moral imperative from another angle. They also use the term "happiness," but for them happiness consists in the life of the spirit in community with friends and in the creative participation in the cognitive and aesthetic values of their culture. The relationship to friends as well as to cultural creativity demands unconditional subjection to the norms and structures of friendship, knowledge, and beauty.

Nearest to Plato's definition of the human *telos* is Aristotle's thought that man's highest aim is participation in the eternal divine self-intuition. This state can be fully reached only by entering the eternal life above finite life. This does not mean that the individual has immortality but that, within time, he can participate in eternity through the "theoretical" life, the life of intuition. Wherever this state of participation is reached, there is *eudaimonia*, fulfillment under the guidance of a "good daimon," a half-divine power. To reach this goal is an unconditional imperative. And since the practical virtues are the precondition for fulfillment through participation in the divine, they also have unconditional validity.

We have used the Greek word *eudaimonia* (badly translated as "happiness") in order to point out the moral aim as described in several ethical schools. *Eudaimonia* belongs to those words that have suffered a marked deterioration in meaning. Most responsible for this process were the Stoic and Christian polemics against Epicureanism, which often unjustly confused Epicureanism with hedonism. The word in itself means fulfillment with divine help, and consequent happiness. This happiness does not exclude pleasure, but the pleasure is not the aim, nor is happiness itself the aim. It is the companion of fulfillment, reached together with it. If we derogate this concept of *eudaimonia*, we must also derogate the Christian hope for eternal blessedness. For, even though the Calvinist names the glory of God as the aim of his life, he experiences blessedness in fulfilling this aim and serving the glory of God. The same, of course, is true of *theosis* ("becoming Godlike"), *fruitio Dei* ("enjoying the intuition of the divine life"), or working for and participating in the "Kingdom of God" described as the aim of the individual man, of mankind, and the universe.

Happiness or blessedness as the emotional awareness of fulfillment is not in conflict with the unconditional, and therefore religious, character of the moral imperative. A conflict exists only when the function of self-transcendence in man's spirit is denied, and man is seen as totally imprisoned in his finitude. But this diminution of man to a finite process has rather rarely occurred in the history of thought. Even highly secularized philosophers were conscious of the function of self-transcendence in man's spirit, and consequently of the dimension of the unconditional or the religious dimension.

There are two concepts in the preceding discussion that have been frequently used without having been thoroughly discussed. The one is "conscience," the channel through which the unconditional character of the moral imperative is experienced, and the other is the term *religious* (in the title and in many other parts of this chapter). The concept of conscience will be fully discussed in Chapter IV. Regarding the concept of religion (which I have developed in much of my work), I can restrict myself to the following summary: The fundamental concept of religion is the state of being grasped by an ultimate concern, by an infinite interest, by something one takes unconditionally seriously. It is in view of this concept that we have formulated the main proposition of this chapter, namely, that there is a religious dimension in the moral imperative itself. Derived from the fundamental concept of religion is the traditional concept that religion is a particular expression, in symbols of thought and action, of such ultimate concern within a social group as, for example, a church. If the moral imperative were derived from religion in the traditional sense of the word, secular ethics would have to sever any ties with religion, for it rejects direct dependence on any particular religion. If, however, the religious element is intrinsic to the moral imperative, no conflict is necessary.

[Reinhold Niebuhr, "The Relevance of the Christian View of Man,"
The Nature and Destiny of Man: A Christian Interpretation
(Louisville: Westminster John Knox Press, 2021), 123–36.]

Individual and General Revelation

The character of Biblical religion must be understood in
contrast to this tendency toward self-immolation in mysticism.
It is a religion that neither reduces the stature of man to the
level of nature nor yet destroys it in an empty and undifferentiated eternity. Biblical religion is variously defined, in
distinction from other religions, as a prophetic or as an apocalyptic religion, or as a religion of revelation. In a religion of
revelation, the unveiling of the eternal purpose and will,
underlying the flux and evanescence of the world, is expected;
and the expectation is fulfilled in personal and social-historical
experience.[1]

From the standpoint of an understanding of human nature,
the significance of a religion of revelation lies in the fact that
both the transcendence of God over, and his intimate relation
to, the world are equally emphasized. He is more completely
transcendent than the eternity of mystic faith. Mysticism
always regards the final depth of human consciousness as in
some sense identical to the eternal order and believes that

91

men may know God if they penetrate deeply enough into the mystery of their own being. But on the other hand, the transcendent God of Biblical faith makes Himself known in the finite and historical world. The finite world is not, because of its finiteness, incapable of entertaining comprehensible revelations of the incomprehensible God. The most important characteristic of a religion of revelation is this two-fold emphasis upon the transcendence of God and upon His intimate relation to the world. In this divine transcendence, the spirit of man finds a home in which it can understand its stature of freedom. But there it also finds the limits of its freedom, the judgment that is spoken against it and, ultimately, the mercy that makes such a judgment sufferable. God's creation of and relation to the world, on the other hand, prove that human finiteness and involvement in flux are essentially good and not evil. A religion of revelation is thus alone able to do justice to both the freedom and the finiteness of man and to understand the character of the evil in him.

The revelation of God to man is always a two-fold one, a personal-individual revelation, and a revelation in the context of social-historical experience. Without the public and historical revelation, the private experience of God would remain poorly defined and subject to caprice. Without the private revelation of God, the public and historical revelation would not gain credence. Since all men have, in some fashion, the experience of a reality beyond themselves, they are able to entertain the more precise revelations of the character and purpose of God as they come to them in the most significant experiences of prophetic history. Private revelation is, in a sense, synonymous with "general" revelation, without the presuppositions of which there could be no "special" revelation. It is no less universal for being private. Private revelation is the testimony in the consciousness of every person whom his life touches—a reality beyond himself, a reality deeper and higher than the system of nature in which he stands.

St. Paul speaks of this experience of God when he declares that even without a further revelation, men are "without excuse" if they do not glorify God as God but become vain in their imagination and make themselves God (Romans 1:20). The experience of God is not so much a separate experience, as an overtone implied in all experience.[2] The soul that reaches the outermost rims of its own consciousness must also come into contact with God, for He impinges upon that consciousness.

Schleiermacher describes this experience of God as the experience of "unqualified dependence." This is one of its aspects, but not its totality. It is one of its aspects because there is, in all human consciousness, at least a dim recognition of the insufficient and dependent character of all finite life, a recognition that implies the consciousness of the reality upon which dependent existence depends. An equally important characteristic of the experience of God is the sense of being seen, commanded, judged, and known from beyond ourselves. This experience is described by the Psalmist in the words "O Lord, thou hast searched me, and known me. Thou knowest my downsitting and mine uprising, . . . and art acquainted with all my ways" (Ps. 139). The Psalmist exults in this relation between God and man and rightly discerns that the greatness and uniqueness of man is as necessary as the greatness of God for such a relationship: "I am fearfully and wonderfully made: marvellous are thy works; and that my soul knoweth right well." If anyone should maintain that this sense of the impingement of God upon human life is a delusion by which man glorifies himself, one might call attention to the fact that in the book of Job exactly the same experience is described by one who is not grateful for it but protests against it. The constant demands and judgments of God seem to him to place life under an intolerable strain: "What is man, that thou shouldest magnify him? and that thou shouldest set thine heart upon him? and that thou shouldest visit him every morning, and try him every moment?" He feels that the divine demands are too exacting for human weakness: "[L]et me alone; for my days are vanity," and he looks forward to the day when death will make the visitations of God impossible: "[F]or now shall I sleep in the dust; and thou shalt seek me in the morning, but I shall not be" (Job 7:16–21). This impious protest against the ever-present accusing God is perhaps a more perfect validation of the reality of the experience than any pious words of gratitude for it.

The experience so described is in some sense identical or associated with what is usually called "conscience." The actual nature of conscience is, of course, variously defined in various philosophies. It may be regarded as the social obligations and judgments that all men must face. Or it may be defined as the obligation and judgment under which the rational or intelligible self places the empirical, the sensible, or the partial self. The significance of the Biblical interpretation of conscience lies precisely in this, that a universal human experience, the sense of being commanded, placed under obligation, and judged, is interpreted as a relation between God and man in which it is God who makes demands and judgments upon man. Such an interpretation of a common experience is not possible without the presuppositions of the Biblical faith. But once accepted, the assumption proves to be the only basis of a correct analysis of all the factors involved in the experience, for it is a fact that man is judged and yet there is no vantage point in his own life, sufficiently transcendent, from which the judgment can take place. St. Paul describes the three levels of judgment under which men stand, and the relativity of all but the last level in the words: "But to me it is a very small thing that I should be judged of you, or of man's judgment: yea, I judge not mine own self. For I know nothing by myself; yet am I not hereby justified: but he that judgeth me is the Lord" (1 Cor. 4:3–4).

It might be argued that the content of a personal experience that can be defined only through the aid of a more historical

revelation of the nature of the divine that enters this experience while this historical revelation can gain credence only
if the personal experience is presupposed, is so involved in
a logical circle as to become incredible. But the fact is that
all human knowledge is also so involved. All common human
experience requires more than the immediate experience to
define the character of the object of experience. The reality
of the object of experience is not in question, but the exact
nature of the reality touched is not clear until it is defined
by insights that transcend the immediate perception of the
object. If the reality touched is something more than a mere
"object" but is itself subject—that is, if its character cannot
be fully revealed to us, except as it takes the initiative—the
principle of interpretation must be something more than
merely the general principles of knowledge that illumine a
particular experience. The principle of interpretation must
be a "revelation."

Our approach to other human personalities offers an illuminating analogy of the necessity and character of "revelation" in our relation to God. We have various evidence that,
when dealing with persons, we are confronting a reality of
greater depth than the mere organism of animal life. We have
evidence that we are dealing with a "Thou" of such freedom
and uniqueness that a mere external observation of its behavior will not only leave the final essence of that person obscure
but will actually falsify it, since such observation would debase
what is really free subject into a mere object. This person, this
other "Thou," cannot be understood until he speaks to us,
until his behavior is clarified by the "word" that comes out
of the ultimate and transcendent unity of his spirit. Only such
a word can give us the key by which we understand the com-
plexities of his behavior. This word spoken from beyond us
and to us is both a verification of our belief that we are dealing
with a different dimension from that of animal existence, and
also a revelation of the actual and precise character of the
person with whom we are dealing.

In the same way, the God whom we meet as "The Other" at the final limit of our own consciousness is not fully known to us except as specific revelations of His character augment this general experience of being confronted from beyond ourselves.

In Biblical faith these specific revelations are apprehended in the context of a particular history of salvation in which specific historical events become special revelations of the character of God and of His purposes. Without the principle of interpretation furnished by this "special revelation," the general experience or the general revelation involved in conscience becomes falsified, because it is explained merely as man's facing the court of social approval or disapproval or as facing his own "best self." In that case, whatever the provisional verdict, the final verdict always is "I know nothing against myself," and the conclusion drawn from this verdict must be and is "I am thereby justified." But this conclusion is at variance with the actual facts of the human situation, for there is no level of moral achievement upon which man can have or actually has an easy conscience.

The fact that a culture which identifies God with some level of human consciousness, either rational or super-rational, or with some order of nature, invariably falsifies the human situation and fails to appreciate either the total stature of freedom in man or the complexity of the problem of evil in him is the most telling negative proof for the Biblical faith. Man does not know himself truly except as he knows himself confronted by God. Only in that confrontation does he become aware of his full stature and freedom and of the evil in him. It is for this reason that Biblical faith is of such importance for the proper understanding of man, and why it is necessary to correct the interpretations of human nature that underestimate his stature, depreciate his physical existence, and fail to deal realistically with the evil in human nature, in terms of Biblical faith.

Creation as Revelation

The general revelation of personal human experience, the sense of being confronted with a "wholly other" at the edge of human consciousness, contains three elements, two of which are not too sharply defined, while the third is not defined at all. The first is the sense of reverence for a majesty and of dependence upon an ultimate source of being. The second is the sense of moral obligation laid upon one from beyond oneself and of moral unworthiness before a judge. The third and most problematic of the elements in religious experience is the longing for forgiveness. All three of these elements become more sharply defined as they gain the support of other forms of revelation. The first, the sense of dependence upon a reality greater and more ultimate than ourselves, gains the support of another form of "general" revelation, the content of which is expressed in the concept of the Creator and the creation. Faith concludes that the same "Thou" who confronts us in our personal experience is also the source and Creator of the whole world. The second element in personal religion, the experience of judgment, gains support from the prophetic-Biblical concept of judgment in history. The whole of history is seen as validation of the truth in the personal experience that God stands over against us as our judge. The third element, the longing for reconciliation after this judgment (and it must be regarded provisionally as a longing rather than an assurance), becomes the great issue of the Old Testament interpretation of life. The question is: Is God merciful as well as just? And if He is merciful, how is His mercy related to His justice? This is the question that hovers over the whole of Biblical religion. Because Christian faith believes the final answer to this ultimate question to be given in Christ, it regards the revelation in Christ as a final revelation, beyond which there can be no further essential revelation. For this reason, it speaks of Christ "as the express image of his person."

Here the whole depth and mystery of the divine are finally revealed.

In these three types of revelation, God becomes specifically defined as Creator, Judge, and Redeemer. It is significant that each term represents a definition of divine transcendence in increasingly specific and sharply delineated terms; and yet in each the relation of God to the world is preserved. They must be studied in order.

To speak of God as Creator of the world is to regard the world in its totality as a revelation of His majesty and self-sufficient power. This revelation still belongs in the category of "general" revelation, though it has been transferred from the inner to the outer world. It is this transfer that St. Paul effects in his argument that "they are without excuse" if "they" do not know God, "because," he declares, "that which may be known of God is manifest *in* them, for God hath showed it unto them." This God who is manifest *in* them further establishes Himself, "for the invisible things of him from the creation of the world are clearly seen, being understood by the things that are made, even his eternal power and Godhead" (Romans 1:19–20). The fact that the world is not self-derived and self-explanatory and self-sufficing but points beyond itself is used as evidence for the doctrine of Creation and to point to the glory of the Creator. In a sense, St. Paul is making use of the cosmological argument at this point, but not in such a way as to be subject to the Kantian criticism. It is not assumed that the reality of God can be proved by the fact that the contingent and dependent character of all finite being implies that the whole of the sensible world "rests upon some intelligible being that is free from all empirical conditions and itself contains the ground of the possibility of all appearances."[3] Rather, the creation is contemplated as pointing to a Creator, already known in man's moral experience. Martin Buber accurately describes the process by which Biblical faith arrives at its concept of the Creator. He says, "The polytheist constructs a god out of every divine appearance, that is, out of every mystery of the world and of existence; but the monotheist recognizes in all these mysteries the same God whom he experienced in personal confrontation. . . . ."[4]

The Biblical doctrine of the Creator, and the world as His creation, is itself not a doctrine of revelation, but it is basic for the doctrine of revelation. It expresses perfectly the basic Biblical idea of both the transcendence of God and His intimate relation to the world. The doctrine is expressed in a "mythical" or supra-rational idea. Genetically the idea of creation is related to primitive concepts in which God is pictured as fashioning the world as the potter molds his clay. The Bible retains this "primitive" concept because it preserves and protects the idea of the freedom of God and His transcendence. These are lost or imperiled by the more rational concept of "first cause" (which takes the place of God in naturalistic philosophies) and by the concept of a form-giving *nous*, which creates by forming the previously formless stuff or matter (which is the basic conception of divinity in idealistic philosophies).

The doctrine of creation preserves the transcendence and freedom of God without implying that the created world is evil because it is not God. On the contrary, Biblical religion consistently maintains the goodness of creation precisely on the ground that it is created by God. In this doctrine of the goodness of creation the foundation is laid for the Biblical emphasis upon the meaningfulness of human history. History is not regarded as evil or meaningless because it is involved in the flux of nature, and man is not regarded as evil because he is dependent upon a physical organism. The doctrine of creation escapes the error of the naturalists who, by regarding causality as the principle of meaning, can find no place for human freedom and are forced to reduce man to the level of nature. It escapes the error of the rationalists who make *nous* into the ultimate principle of meaning and are thereby tempted to divide man into an essentially good reason, which participates in or is identified with the divine, and an essentially evil physical life.

To reject the principle of natural causation as the final principle of interpreting the unity of the world is not to interpret the world merely from the standpoint of man's internal problem or to read psychic attributes of man into nature. The fact is that the relation of things to each other in the chain of natural causation is not an adequate explanation of their specific givenness. This irrational givenness must be regarded either as merely chance or caprice, or the order of the world must be related to a more ultimate realm of freedom. There is, in other words, a gain for an adequate cosmology if man uses concepts in his interpretations of the cosmos that he won first of all in measuring the dimension of his own internal reality. Even nature is better understood if it is measured in a dimension of depth that is initially suggested by the structure of human consciousness and by the experience of a reality more ultimate than his own that impinges upon his freedom.

In the same manner, the doctrine of creation corrects mistakes in rationalistic and idealistic cosmologies. These cosmologies are forced to presuppose some unformed stuff, some realm of chaos, which *nous* fashions into order, and to identify this forming process with creation. The Biblical doctrine of creation derives both the formless stuff and the forming principle from a more ultimate divine source, which it defines as both *logos* and as creative will, as both the principle of form and the principle of vitality. The supra-rational character of this doctrine is proved by the fact that, when pressed logically, it leads to the assertion that God creates *ex nihilo*, the idea at which all logical concepts of derivation must end—and begin.

The only metaphysical system that can be compared with the Biblical idea of Creator and creation, in terms of the dimension of depth that it assigns to the world is the system of mysticism. One may speak of a mystical metaphysics because there is a remarkable unity and unanimity in mystical interpretations of life and reality, whether they develop in East or

West and whether it be Plotinus or Buddha who elaborates the philosophy in detail. In all of them the finite world is regarded as illusory, or evil; in all of them the eternal world is regarded as a realm of undifferentiated unity from which the particularity, individuality, and insufficiency of the finite world have been expunged; all of them place *nous, logos,* reason, or form, which for the rationalists represents the eternal principle within flux, into the category of the finite, while they seek a more ultimate and undifferentiated unity than "contrasting thoughts"; all of them seek to arrive at this unity of the divine and eternal by a rigorous discipline of introversion which assumes that the unity of consciousness above the level of sense experience but also above the level of reason is identical with the divine. Brahman and Atman are one.

Mysticism, which is therefore closest to Biblical religion in measuring the depth of reality and the height of human consciousness, is also in sharpest contrast to the Biblical concept of Creator and creation. The contrast is threefold. (1) In contrast to the creative will and wisdom of the divine in the Biblical conception of God, it defines God in terms of negation.[5] (2) In contrast to the Biblical doctrine of the goodness of creation, the finite, differentiated, and particularized world is regarded as either illusory or evil. The human ego, as finite and particularized reality, is evil by virtue of its being an ego; and salvation consists essentially in the destruction of individuality. (3) Despite this ultimate destruction of individuality, mysticism makes for a provisional deification of man, because it believes that God is identical to the deepest level of human consciousness. This is in contrast to the Biblical doctrine of the creatureliness of man and to the sharp Biblical distinction between Creator and creature.

The Biblical doctrine of Creator and creation is thus the only ground upon which the full height of the human spirit can be measured, the unity of its life in body and soul be maintained, and the essential meaningfulness of its history in

the finite world asserted, and a limit set for its freedom, and
self-transcendence.

Notes

1. Oman defines the difference between mystical and
apocalyptic religions as follows: "In the former case the eternal
is sought as the unchanging by escape from the evanescent; in
the latter it is looked for in the evanescent as a revelation of the
increasing purpose in its changes." . . . "A mystical religion is,
as it should always be understood scientifically, one that seeks
the eternal behind the illusion of the evanescent; but in using
'apocalyptic' for any religion which looks for a revealing in the
evanescent the term is extended from its customary use, which is
for a religion which expects this in sudden catastrophic form, to
one which expects it in any form." *The Natural and the Super-
natural*, pp. 403–409.

2. John Baillie writes very truly: "No matter how far back
I go, no matter by what effort of memory I attempt to reach the
virgin soil of childish innocence, I cannot get back to an atheistic
mentality. As little can I reach a day when I was conscious of myself
but not of God as I can reach a day when I was conscious of myself
but not of other human beings." *Our Knowledge of God*, p. 4.

3. Immanuel Kant, *Critique of Pure Reason*, Book II, Ch. ii,
par. 4.

4. Martin Buber, *Koenigtum Gottes* (Heidelberg: L. Schneider,
1956) p. 91.

5. Mercer in *Nature Mysticism* describes the mystic process of
defining the eternal and divine as follows: "By a ruthless process of
abstraction they have abjured the world of sense to vow allegiance
to a mode of being about which nothing can be said without
denying it . . . it embraces everything and remains pure negation—
leave us not alone with the absolute of orthodox mysticism lest we
perish of inanition" (p. 10). Rufus Jones recognizes this tendency
in mysticism but, like most Christian mystics, he regards it as an
aberration rather than as a constitutional weakness of mysticism.
Studies in Mystical Religion, Ch. 6.

III

Enlightened Spirituality
in Post-Enlightenment Cultures

We do not live in the intellectual culture of the Enlightenment philosophers. The world has become both larger and smaller, and enough has changed for many to refer to the present as postmodern. But that hardly means that themes that emerged then and are displayed in this work of Immanuel Kant have lost all relevance. The situation is much more complicated. The churches still use the languages of the thirteenth and sixteenth centuries in their theologies of the Christian life. At the same time, the developed Western societies take many Enlightenment values for granted and thus invite enlightened criticism. Upon reflection, aside from the rote familiarity of the words, much of premodern Christian spirituality does not really make sense. This reflection aims at raising to the surface some of the fundamental values enshrined in Kantian ethics to show how they may help people to better understand Christian life today.

The perspective for this commentary stands firmly in the present moment; one cannot go back. Today's culture begs for attention to what unifies the Christian life in the pluralism that abounds, and for respect for the distinctiveness of discrete subcultures and the individuals within them. It eschews the universal as discriminatory and prejudicial. But reductionism on any side of a question usually misses the mark. What is aimed for here is not strictly Kantian; we have moved on, and the perspective has become wider. It helps to recall that Kant was a philosopher and not a theologian; in the end, Kant's view of Christian faith was somewhat reductionist.

As a final pre-note, the sources for this commentary are limited. Much more could be said about God, the peculiar knowledge of God that is faith, Kant's work in aesthetics, and the social interpretation of the rule of God that had so much influence in the following centuries. But Kant forces reflection, that unique ability of human beings, on the suppositions of everyday life. At that level he occasions new insights for our time. These are not presented in the form of a central thesis with corollaries but as a series of distinct observations that emerge out of Kant's transcendental method.

Finding Transcendent Meaning

A first lesson for spirituality that one could learn from Immanuel Kant relates to the place where people find transcendent meaning. Contemporary postmodern life poses the question in the face of the way science explains everything through analysis of empirical data and thus implicitly reduces human self-understanding to a form of functional analysis. Evolutionary psychology, for example, has a reductionist tendency written into its assumptions. We can explain ourselves by the many forces that created us; an individual act of freedom can be understood by its antecedents. Social conditioning of commonplace assumptions seems to condemn the human race to relativism. The same forces that were operative within Enlightenment culture have been generalized and compounded into an implicit cultural cynicism that does not trust any language of transcendence. We begin by addressing the question of where one can find any trustworthy transcendent meaning in today's intellectual culture.

Kant's response to this question lies within the context of his philosophical thinking, which consisted of transcendental analysis of human subjectivity.[1] Kant falls within the tradition of transposing the focus of philosophical analysis from observation of external phenomena to an examination of human response. In terms of a philosophical tradition, this relates him to Descartes. In terms of spiritual writers, this places Kant with those who maintain that the ultimate answer to the quest for God will be found within the human subject itself: "*Deus interior intimo meo.*"[2] Kant, of course, is not known as a spiritual writer, but his critical philosophy draws attention to human subjectivity as the "place" where experience of God, or consciousness of God, begins to make sense.

Kant was a Christian; he professed faith in God. But in his view, faith and knowledge were distinct, because proper knowledge requires sensible data. But he plants the encounter with God within the human subject, not as an object of empirical experience, which it could not be, but as the necessary entailment of an unconditional experience of responsibility. Such a conviction of faith is actually a different kind of knowledge, and it furnishes an all-encompassing meaningfulness to human experience itself. This is the "place" where God can be encountered (Kant said "postulated"),[3] and it is entailed within the human experience of moral obligation. What Kant named a categorical imperative calls forth, in turn, a self-transcendence and responsibility that open human subjectivity to a sphere of reality that is truly ultimate, spiritual, and transcendent relative to the individual and society. God is found within us not as a clear and distinct idea but as buried in a common essential experience of a person in society: I am free and therefore responsible, and this is inescapable. God is experienced by indirection within that complex of human subjectivity as that which is entailed in the absolute character of an inner moral imperative.

God Is on Our Side

In attacking religious authority in society, the Enlightenment seemed to be attacking the very notion of God as alienating. Tillich helps to sort things out here. He clearly reminds us that morality and ethics do not depend on religion; he reinforces Kant's analysis that morality springs from the depths of human existence itself. Morality cannot be alienating, because it finds its roots in the freedom and autonomy of the human person that must be respected. But then Tillich turns the insight inside-out: "[T]he religious dimension of the moral imperative is its unconditional character."[3] It does not lie in the first place in specific content, in doing this or doing that. The will of God does not dictate the concrete human decisions that people make as in an external code of behavior. The will of God, therefore, "is not an external will imposed upon us, an arbitrary law laid down by a heavenly tyrant": It is, rather, "precisely our essential being with all its potentialities, our created nature" that God created as good. "For us the 'Will of God' is manifest in our essential being; and only because of this can we accept the moral imperative as valid."[4] Here lies a basic principle for modern spirituality. The fundamental perspective moves the human spirit from feelings of the alienation of freedom to an autonomy that is affirmed and safeguarded. Tillich called this "theonomy," a being supported in one's freedom in such a way that the freedom of others is respected.

Finding Universal Meaning

The question of whether one can find transcendent meaning that is universal and not simply private relates to values rather than to facts. "Value" refers to the quality of things, their importance and goodness. In Kant's search for the norms for the good, the subject matter transcends empirical data. We are looking for intrinsic worth. The issue transcends empirical facts. For example, the discovery of heliocentrism or whether or not the human evolved from simpler forms of life at first seemed to, but does not really, undermine the value of the human person. Today we are used to a plurality of values across history and in the contemporary world. But to say that racism is wrong today but was not so in the past cuts across the grain. It makes more sense to say that other people were ignorant or their thinking was limited or askew. The idea of "truth for me" or that deep value depends on the culture in place rankles the sense of belonging to a single species with a fundamental desire to know the truth and not be misled. When it comes to the fundamental meaning of human existence itself, true value seems far more important than true facts. We cannot help but think that there must be some universal basis for equity.

An important fundamental contribution to a postmodern spirituality provided by Kant's response to the question of a universal norm for the good lay in how he defined it. He did not find it in a specific command to do this or that but in a formal principle that hedged in the options. The universality was not found in the action to be done, or who did it and when, but in its formal character that precisely transcended particular history and circumstance. He found the norm for the good within human reflection itself. His argument is intuitive and almost tautological: If you want to be sure you are conforming to universal good, do only that which to the best of your ability seems to be good universally. An inner sense of justice and rightness that Kant called the categorical imperative impels this. And, as Tillich commented, it is unconditional.

The spiritual relevance of Kant's conviction shines against the dark background of the disenchanted secular world that some think is represented to us by the sciences. They force us to think empirically and instrumentally; they turn our outlook away from special overt manifestations of God in the world, as, for example, in miracles, or even in a single incarnation that exclusively accounts for the salvation of all. But, at the same time, Christians have to find a domain that is universal and wherein the salvation of God is offered to all. This impels the person of faith to look for God within the human spirit, and to do so in such a way that God can be encountered by everyone. This by no means rules out a historical incarnation and revelation because all human experience transpires in a historical context, revelation included. Rather, the categorical imperative impels Christians to think of God's acting in all human beings in a way analogous to how they find God working in their own experience. The universality of this principle means that the plurality of religions does not compete with Christian faith and thus undermine it but reinforces and thus confirms its transcendental meaningfulness.

Ultimate reality is experienced differently among all peoples because all are shaped by and responsive to particular historical sets of experience and traditions. In fact, all people need a historical sign to identify the nature of ultimacy as they encounter it. Jesus thus stands at the center of Christian faith, and he occupies that place because Christians look to him as the revelation of the nature of the God, who is found within all human beings in ways that are distinct from other, different religious traditions. This function does not in itself exhaust a Christian spirituality, but it forms part of the foundation for the metaphysics of Christian spirituality.

The Role of Jesus in Christian Spirituality

The question of the role of Jesus in Christian spirituality may be too large and too delicate to discuss in such a limited framework, but the theme is not new, and something can be said that is distinctive to Kant. Kant clearly raises two questions for traditional Christian spirituality. In the *Metaphysics for Morals* he explicitly denies that morality can be rooted in external examples. But the following of Christ reflects a longstanding tradition of spirituality from Christian beginnings and is exemplified in the *Imitatio Christi* of Thomas à Kempis. In *Religion within the Limits of Reason Alone*, Kant depicts the moral teaching of Jesus, including his teaching on the kingdom of God, as a positive historical form of the universal ethics of human responsibility and the eschatological kingdom of ends.[5] Without justifying Kant's reasoning on those issues, a constructive interpretation of certain aspects of his views offers positive support for Christian spirituality today.

First of all, the simple reflection frequently offered in Christian catechesis relative to the commandments helps in the appreciation of the level at which Kant approaches morality and by extension spirituality. The teacher asks the student, is murder wrong because it is forbidden, or is it forbidden because it is wrong? The question mediates Kant's insight and draws the mind to a new level of understanding. Critical reasoning does not undermine morality but elicits a deeper understanding of the sphere that gives rise to its meaningfulness. Of course, Christians follow Jesus because he presents to them in the most concrete way the moral dynamics of human existence. Jesus mediates the will of God to Christian consciousness by way of example. Kant distinguished his categorical imperative from Jesus's teaching of the Golden Rule and from external authority: It is an essential part of transcendental subjectivity. But the categorical imperative brought home the teaching of Jesus for an enlightened audience. The following of Jesus does not consist of mimicry but of finding Jesus's inner principle within the self.

To address so briefly Kant's view of the role of Jesus in Christian spirituality is surely inadequate, but it is not inappropriate to make a constructive point that relates to Christian spirituality today. Kant viewed Jesus Christ and the scripture in which he is represented as the basis of Christian self-understanding and spirituality. But he also realized that those historical data had to be appropriated in each age. For Kant, rational religion, or the religion of pure reason, provided the definitive meaning of historical beliefs and morals.[6] Apart from the confidence of a bygone age, and in the light of a historical and pluralistic consciousness, Kant's insistence that positive religious traditions have to be constantly criticized by the reason of the age makes perfect sense. That dynamic constitutes the living substance of Christian theology, ethics, and spirituality. Historical consciousness does not negate transcendental method but accompanies it.

But Kant's view of reason was itself historically conditioned. He was not a student of other religions. His thinking was narrowly Christian in terms of faith traditions. His appeal to the abstract universal represents his strength, but he does not communicate how deep and thorough are the influences of history on the mechanisms of the mind, even those of the enlightened mind. Reason itself always bears the marks of history, and common content across cultures can be identified, but not easily. When intrinsic reasons for pluralism are recognized, they strengthen Kant's formula that requires the continual interpretation of belief, moral behavior, and spirituality. Within this framework, Jesus Christ retains his place at the center of Christian faith in God as its mediator. But our present larger horizon calls for more openness to other historical encounters with God. In Kant's thinking, the foundation for the metaphysics of specifically Christian spirituality lies deeply embedded in the categorical imperative and in Jesus's teaching of unity of love of God and love of neighbor. Today that same metaphysics enables the Christian to recognize that the spiritualities of other religions that reflect how love of God and love of neighbor imply each other can also be true and authentic.

On Religious Authority

A discussion of the Enlightenment and of Kant's thought relative to religious authority teems with tensions. In some ways the very meaning of enlightenment is illuminated by authoritarianism, mainly of the churches and their traditions, to which it stood opposed. The antitheses are a commonplace: faith and reason, sacred and profane, church and state, authority and free thinking. These couplings do not represent a balance in common perception; the two sides are antithetical, frequently refer to extremes, and compete for allegiance. The previous reflection suggested that they can get along with each other and that Kant suggested a dated but intrinsically positive formula for their complementarity. But it requires a fundamentally different notion of religious authority from the way it was and largely still is understood.

Kant represents a view in which authority, in the deep matters of truth, morals, spirituality, and religion, is not antithetical to reason but contained in and carried *by* reason. The relationship of human beings to God manifests itself implicitly within a universal moral sensibility. On the surface of human affairs, Kant would agree with Luther and Calvin that law consisted of social provisions for the common good. It orders society, in some measure controls corporate behavior, and protects life. But he would not agree with Calvin when he thought of the church as the exclusive voice of God's authority. In Calvin's thought, God could have dealt but did not deal with each person by a universal yet discrete mechanism. He wrote, "[A]lthough God's power is not bound to outward means, he has nonetheless bound us to this ordinary manner of teaching."[7] In Kant, God is not the author of positive laws. In a way, this pinpoints the revolution of the Enlightenment that Kant made explicit. God's authority may be reflected in the church, but at the same time God's authority can be encountered within every person, and moral sensibility exemplifies such an experience. This potentially universal experience as Kant understood it certainly contradicted the church teachings of the time. But such an antithesis and the competitive suppositions upon which it lies do not have universal Christian support today. Increasingly, theologians read God's gracious saving activity in the world at large much more generously and invite the churches to attend to the cultures they address.

The very nature of authority and law seems crucial to this discussion. At this juncture the question penetrates below the surface of a common understanding of authority and law as extrinsicist or originating outside of human subjectivity. Authority in that case appears as essentially limiting, directing, and controlling freedom. In Kant's view, God's will is not laid upon us from outside ourselves but is discovered within our deepest self. In the religious sphere, this means that religious experience and response are intrinsically rational. Faith and participation in some form of ultimacy does not diminish human intelligence, freedom, and autonomy but expands them. The insight transforms the sphere of religious authority. Instead of being heteronomous, recognizing authority within religious consciousness expands the meaning and the being itself of human existence. Freedom receives an importance and scope that it could not dream of without connection to the absolute reality of God that makes such value possible.

In sum, to make this point explicit, God's authority over human freedom does not consist in heteronomously binding law; it appears in an internal experience of responsibility; it is not imposed coercively but appeals suasively to human freedom as that which will fulfill all that is positive in human existence.

Dependence on God as Empowerment

Dependence on God does not debilitate but empowers human freedom. This statement is a corollary to the authority of God that can be found implicit in moral sensibility. It goes beyond the framework of consciousness to the ontology of freedom and the theology of grace. It reaches beyond the idea of authority to the fundamental basis of spirituality itself. In this approach through the human subject to the spiritual domain, God appears less as an external lawgiver curtailing freedom and more as the sustainer and curator of human existence. In God, one finds the ground and guarantor of the value of the human person and the human project that is carried forward by human freedom. In this experience of dependence, closeness to God does not translate into submission to external power or obedience to a law that suppresses human agency. The opposite is the case. Human existence is more fully human and freedom is more fully empowered by closer connection with the ground of existence itself and the guarantor of its value.

The key to this seeming paradox of freedom in dependence does not lie in a balance of like forces. One cannot understand the being and action of God as if God were another creature competing with human energy. God sustains human freedom as autonomous creativity in its own finite context. This becomes newly significant in a newly secularized world. This deeper religious interpretation of the ground of spirituality can be found in different ways underlying the spirituality of grace in Aquinas, Luther's spirituality of gratitude, Calvin's spirituality of sanctification, and Wesley's spirituality of feeling in response to the inner Spirit of God. Commitment to God and to the human project do not contend with each other as in a zero-sum relationship: God's grace versus human freedom. Jesus reveals the ultimate within human subjectivity as a benevolent and saving presence that is entirely pro-human.

The Duality of Christian Responsibility

How do the churches represent the creativity and freedom of Christian spirituality within society? Institutions tend to hoard whatever social power they possess. The churches enjoyed a great deal of authority in the early modern period in Europe. They did not welcome the Enlightenment. For their part, the *illuminati* as a movement experienced the churches as authoritarian and hostile to science, modern philosophy, and social and political creativity. It is one thing to interpret the relevance of Christian faith for personal and corporate spirituality, but it is another thing entirely to envision how that spiritual potential manifests itself in the Christian churches that often appear to behave as instinctively traditional and conservative institutions.[8]

In the face of Christian institutional authoritarianism, Christian spirituality involves a dual responsibility of obedience to God and to the substance of human existence. Kant's internalization of the experience of God's authority understands that an ethics of obedience to the will of God includes an ethics of empowerment to engage the human project in genuine hope. Obedience no longer operates by an infantile logic of command and blind obedience to an external authority. Obedience, as a response to an appeal from within human nature and subjectivity, calls people to transcend immediate personal satisfaction and attend to values that are within but come from beyond the self. Since these same values transcend all our selves together, and thus society, they are precisely religious. In this construal, all the themes that describe the thought of Immanuel Kant are transformed and given a new, positive constructive meaning: Christian faith, rational faith, law, obedience, and the rule of God. They come from God as creator and sustaining ground, but they also announce essentially human values and tasks. God remains absolute mystery in all of this, but these symbols call up something that is real and experienced, not directly, but indirectly within the person.

Sin and Judgment

Finally, where does this picture of Christian spirituality locate sin and God's judgment upon it? A response to this question in Kantian terms, even in its simplest terms, involves layers of Kant's vision of things. The knowledge that faith generates has at least two distinct dimensions: It is historically mediated and is rational and spiritual. The historical dimension consists of the positive situation and data that give rise to any religious movement or person in it: a historical beginning and the positive content mediated by historical revelation. The spiritual side of religion is found in the deep structure of a rational response to the God illustrated in a categorical moral imperative. It makes no sense to separate the rational and the spiritual: Inner spiritual freedom engages rational human reflection.[9] The distinction between the historical and the rational/spiritual can be read in this contrast: "Pure religious faith alone can found a universal church; for only [such] rational faith can be believed in and shared by everyone, whereas an historical faith, grounded solely on facts, can extend its influence no further than tidings of it can reach. . . ."[10]

Kant recognized the particularity of historical existence, the evil that infects history, and the debility of human nature. These conditions affect everyone's ability to possess a pure religious faith and spirituality that relate solely to God. In short, human beings generally need external support and the organization of a positive, tangible historical religious society. Only through gradual critique will positive historical religiosity give way to the enlightened critique of pure reason. This does not separate popular and critical religion and spirituality, but it provides a spectrum of faith life that is more or less self-critical.

In Kant's view, Christianity represents the highest and penultimate form of religion that actually contains within itself pure rational religious faith. This vision of religion within the limits of reason lacks something that appears relatively obvious to the observer at the beginning of the twenty-first century, after two world wars, the programmatic effort to eradicate all Jews from Europe, the use of nuclear weaponry, and an abundance of smaller wars with sophisticated means of killing and open unconcern about the loss of life. Twenty-first-century hindsight, with an enhanced historical and social consciousness, cannot ignore the repeated systematic suppression of whole groups of people. There has never been such a wholesale manifestation of the damaged character of human existence than what can be perceived in the world today. There simply has never been such massive hunger, disease, and violence in the history of the human race, and it directly attacks the conviction that human life enjoys some measure of absolute value. How strong is the categorical imperative that human beings should not be used as merely a means? Where is the dialectical imagination that recognizes God's righteous condemnation of human sin? Kant seems to have had no strong sense of God's standing in judgment of human self-interest, or of God's being affected by the suffering that human beings inflict on so many, mainly through social mechanisms that benefit some at the expense of so many others.

This dimension of ourselves, individually and corporately, has to command more attention of Christian rational spiritual response. At this point, the salutary realism in Niebuhr's depiction of an accusatory dimension of a transcendent moral obligation comes to the fore. Niebuhr believed that general revelation is mediated through conscience; or, conscience plays a role in fundamental religious experience. But it has a dialectical character: God enters our consciousness from the outside as judge. Religious consciousness has two dimensions: "The first is the sense of reverence for a majesty and of dependence upon an ultimate source of being. The second is the sense of moral obligation laid upon one from beyond oneself and of moral unworthiness before a judge."[11] In this second dimension the role of conscience modifies the moral or categorical imperative analyzed by Kant and adds a negative structural dimension. "The whole of history is seen as validation of the truth in the personal experience that God stands over against us as our judge."[12] In this view of things, the fundamental idea of creation is mediated through this moral sense. The doctrine of creation "is contemplated as pointing to a Creator, already known in man's moral experience."[13] The stress falls on God's otherness and transcendence that manifest themselves as including a dimension of moral judgment.

Today's statistics of human suffering are staggering, and most of it does not come from natural disasters but is humanly caused or tolerated. The dialectical character of the Reformation's conception of God's standing against human depravity has to find a place in Christian spirituality. Moral sensibility today reacts against the dehumanizing aspects of society. It detects a deeper moral weakness in each individual that gives rise to the social dilemmas that human beings are incapable of fixing. Kant brilliantly describes a common personal moral sensibility that can be found in all human beings. But he does not give an adequate account of moral cynicism on the one hand or, on the other hand, the outrage at the fact that whole groups of people have been consistently marginalized and dehumanized. He does not speak to vast sectors of society who are innocent victims of the narrowly rational systems that human beings have constructed.

To sum up this commentary, Immanuel Kant has helped us to probe the transcendental grounds of spirituality and its moral depths. He brings us back to the inner sources of religious experience that subvert a sense of alienation. Tillich accents Kant's lesson that, when God is found within human experience itself, God will reappear as the ground of our individual autonomy. And Reinhold Niebuhr, who thought about humanity in social terms, adds to a Kantian analysis the dimension of God as judge who holds humanity accountable for massive social dehumanization. As Christian history began to take deep roots outside of Europe, and as the so-called Enlightenment spread to new times and cultures, Christian spirituality expanded its horizons well beyond eighteenth-century European culture. Christian spirituality has learned from the negative experiences of dehumanization. New experiences of evil provide new demands for redress

and salvation that can come only from an ultimate ground
that ensures justice in the end and also stands in judgment
against corporate sin now.

Notes

1. The significance of Kant's turn to the subject in his philosophy
is prior to any discussion of how the categorical imperative relates
to a religious consciousness or conscience. This later question is
most important for understanding spirituality and will be engaged
further on.

2. God, Augustine wrote, was "more inward to me than my
most inward part." *Confessions*, 3.6.11.

3. Paul Tillich, "The Religious Dimension of the Moral
Imperative, *Morality and Beyond* (New York: Harper Torchbooks,
1963), 22.

4. Tillich, *Morality and Beyond*, 24.

5. Kant depicts the ethical commonwealth as the people of
God—that is, God as the moral ruler of the world and a people of
God under divine commands: not external statutory laws as in a
theocracy, but the inner laws of virtue. This people of God stands
as a unity against the rabble of the evil principle. Immanuel Kant,
Religion within the Limits of Reason Alone, trans. T. M. Greene
and H. H. Hudson (New York: Harper Torchbooks, 1960),
90–91. This is reminiscent of but not dependent upon Ignatius
Loyola's "Two Standards" in his Spiritual Exercises.

6. Kant, *Religion within the Limits of Reason Alone*, 94–114.
In today's culture, marked by radical historical consciousness,
the very idea that a society can finally come of age seems like an
adolescent boast.

7. John Calvin, *Calvin: Institutes of the Christian Religion*
(Philadelphia: Westminster Press, 1960), Book 4, Chap. 1, Para. 5,
p. 1018. The text illustrates the principle in Calvin that the church,
positive religion, is the medium or external means of salvation.

8. Broad generalizations such as this require distinctions
among denominational traditions, subject matters, and historical
circumstances that blunt but do not remove the edges of the
criticism.

9. Associating spirituality and rationality does not mean an inability to differentiate between myriad human responses to the world, but it suggests that the idea of "rationality" cannot itself be reduced to a narrow form of activity. Rationality traditionally characterizes the human person and points to a self-reflective dimension that suffuses all human responses in some measure and to some degree.

10. Kant, *Religion within the Limits of Reason Alone*, 94.

11. Reinhold Niebuhr, *The Nature and Destiny of Man. I. Human Nature* (New York: Charles Scribner's Sons, 1964), 131.

12. Niebuhr, *The Nature and Destiny of Man*, 132.

13. Niebuhr, *The Nature and Destiny of Man*, 133.

Further Reading

Allison, Henry E. *Essays on Kant*. Oxford: Oxford University Press, 2012 (online). [Allison covers many basic ideas of Kant's philosophy in an accessible way. His brief chapter "Kant's Conception of Aufklärung" is very helpful in situating Kant's perspective.]

Brown, Charles C. *Niebuhr and His Age: Reinhold Niebuhr's Prophetic Role in the Twentieth Century*. Philadelphia: Trinity Press, 1992, 2002. [This book introduces the reader to the life of Niebuhr and then analyzes the development of his thought as a theologian, social ethicist, and political commentator.]

Fox, Richard W. *Reinhold Niebuhr: A Biography*. Ithaca, NY: Cornell University Press, 1966. [Fox writes an accessible and insightful portrait of the life and career of Reinhold Niebuhr, although thinkers close to Niebuhr disagreed with some of Fox's judgments.]

Gilkey, Langdon. *Gilkey on Tillich*. New York: Crossroad, 1990. [A cultural theologian gives his personal and theological appreciation of a mentor who influenced him greatly.]

Lovin, Robert, and Joshua Mauldin, eds. *The Oxford Handbook of Reinhold Niebuhr*. Oxford: Oxford University Press, 2021 (online). [This handbook is very thorough in representing the times and problems faced by Niebuhr over the course of his career and his signature social moral realism.]

Re Manning, Russell. *The Cambridge Companion to Paul Tillich*. Cambridge: Cambridge University Press, 2009 (online). [This volume contains eighteen essays on basic elements of Tillich's work, including a short description of his life and authorship;

his theology in relation to culture, ethics, and other religions; and his sermons as a place to enter his world.]

Scruton, Roger. *Kant*. Oxford, New York: Oxford University Press, 1982. [This short book introduces the philosophy of Immanuel Kant in an expertly concise and accessible way.]

Wood, Allen W. "Rational Theology, Moral Faith, and Religion," in *The Cambridge Companion to Kant*, ed. Paul Guyer. Cambridge and New York: Cambridge University Press, 1992 (online, 2006): 394–416. [This short chapter provides basic insights that Wood develops at greater length in *Kant and Religion*. Cambridge: Cambridge University Press, 2020 (online). He places moral faith in God in a wider context of Kant's *Religion within the Limits of Reason Alone*.]

Wood, Allen W. *Kantian Ethics*. Cambridge: Cambridge University Press, 2008 (online). [This is an excellent source for examining more carefully reason, the moral law, autonomy, freedom, and conscience in Kant's thinking.]

About the Series

The volumes of this series provide readers direct access to important voices in the history of the faith. Each of the writings has been selected, first, for its value as a historical document that captures the cultural and theological expression of a figure's encounter with God. Second, as "classics," the primary materials witness to the "transcendent" in a way that has proved potent for the formation of Christian life and meaning beyond the particularities of the setting of its authorship.

Recent renewed interest in mysticism and spirituality have encouraged new movements, contributed to a growing body of therapeutic-moral literature, and inspired the recovery of ancient practices from Church tradition. However, the meaning of the notoriously slippery term "spirituality" remains contested. The many authors who write on the topic have different frameworks of reference, divergent criteria of evaluation, and competing senses of the principal sources or witnesses. This situation makes it important to state the operative definition used in this series. *Spirituality is the way people live in relation to what they consider to be ultimate.* So defined, spirituality is a universal phenomenon: everyone has one, whether they can fully articulate it or not. Spirituality emphasizes lived experience and concrete expression of one's principles, attitudes, and convictions, whether rooted in a defined tradition or not. It includes not only interiority and devotional practices but also the real outworkings of people's ideas and values. Students of spirituality examine the way that a person or group conceives of a meaningful existence through the practices that orient them toward their horizon of deepest meaning. What animates their life? What motivates their truest desires? What sustains them and instructs them? What provides for them a vision of the good life? How do they define and pursue truth? And how do they imagine and work to realize their shared vision of a good society?

The "classic" texts and authors presented in these volumes, though they represent the diversity of Christian traditions, define their ultimate value in God through Christ by the Spirit. They share a conviction that the Divine has revealed God's self in history through Jesus Christ. God's self-communication, in turn, invites a response through faith to participate in an intentional life of self-transcendence and to co-labor with the Spirit in manifesting the reign of God. Thus, *Christian spirituality refers to the way that individuals or social entities live out their encounter with God in Jesus Christ by a life in the Spirit.*

Christian spirituality necessarily involves a hermeneutical task. Followers of Christ set about the work of integrating knowledge and determining meaning through an interpretative process that refracts through different lenses: the life of Jesus, the witness of the scripture, the norms of the faith community, the traditions and social structures of one's heritage, the questions of direct experience, the criteria of the academy and other institutions that mediate truthfulness and viability, and personal conscience. These seemingly competing authorities can leave contemporary students of theology with more quandaries than clarity. Thus, this series has anticipated this challenge with an intentional structure that will guide students through their encounter with classic texts. Rather than providing commentary on the writings themselves, this series invites the audience to engage the texts with an informed sense of the context of their authorship and a dialog with the text that begins a conversation about how to make the text meaningful for theology, spirituality, and ethics in the present.

Most of the readers of these texts will be familiar with critical historical methods which enable an understanding of scripture in the context within which it was written. However, many people read scripture according to the common sense understanding of their ordinary language. This almost inevitably leads to some degree of misinterpretation. The Bible's content lies embedded in its cultural context, which is foreign to the experience of contemporary believers. Critical historical study enables a reader to get closer to an authentic past meaning by explicitly attending to the historical period, the situation of the author, and other particularities of the composition of the text. For example, one would miss the point of the story of the "Good Samaritan" if one did not recognize that the first-century Palestinian conflict between Jews and Samaritans makes the hero of the Jewish parable an enemy and an unlikely model of virtue! Something deeper than a simple offer of neighborly love is going on in this text.

However, the more exacting the critical historical method becomes, the greater it increases the distance between the text and the present-day reader. Thus, a second obstacle to interpreting classics for contemporary theology, ethics, and spirituality lies in a bias that texts embedded in a world so different from today cannot carry an inner authority for present life. How can we find something both true and relevant for faith today in a witness that a critical historical method determines to be in some measure alien? The basic problem has two dimensions: how do we appreciate the past witnesses of our tradition on their own terms, and, once we have, how can we learn from something so dissimilar?

Most Christians have some experience navigating this dilemma through biblical interpretation. Through Church membership, Christians have gained familiarity with scriptural language, and preaching consistently applies its content to daily life. But beyond the Bible, a long history of cultural understanding, linguistic innovation, doctrinal negotiations, and shifting patterns of practices has added layer upon layer of meaning to Christian spirituality. Veiled in unfamiliar grammar, images, and politics, these texts may appear as cultural artifacts suitable only for scholarly treatments. How can a modern student of theology understand a text cloaked in an unknown history and still encounter in it a transcendent faith that animates life in the present? Many historical and theological aspects of Christian spirituality that are still operative in communities of faith are losing traction among swathes of the population, especially younger generations. Their premises have been called into question; the metaphors are dead; the symbols appear unable to mediate grace; and the ideas appear untenable. For example, is the human species really saved by the blood of Jesus on the cross? What does it mean to be resurrected from the dead? How does the Spirit unify if the church is so divided? On the other hand, the positive experiences and insights that accrued over time and added depth to Christian spirituality are being lost because they lack critical appropriation for our time. For example, has asceticism been completely lost in present-day spirituality or can we find meaning for it today? Do the mystics live in another universe, or can we find mystical dimensions in religious consciousness today? Does monasticism bear meaning for those who live outside the walls?

This series addresses these questions with a three-fold strategy. The historical first step introduces the reader to individuals who represent key ideas, themes, movements, doctrinal developments, or remarkable distinctions in theology, ethics, or spirituality. This first section will equip readers with a sense of the context of the authorship and a grammar for understanding the text.

Second, the reader will encounter the witnesses in their own words. The selected excerpts from the authors' works have exercised great influence in the history of Christianity. Letting these texts speak for themselves will enable readers to encounter the wisdom and insight of these classics anew. Equipped with the necessary background and language from the introduction, students of theology will bring the questions and concerns of their world into contact with the world of the authors. This move personalizes the objective historical context and allows the existential character of the classic witness to appear. The goal is not the study of the exact meaning of ancient texts, as important as that is. That would require a task outside the scope of this series. Recommended readings will be provided for those who wish to continue digging into this important part of interpretation. These classic texts are not presented as comprehensive representations of their authors but as statements of basic characteristic ideas that still have bearing on lived experience of faith in the twenty-first century. The emphasis lies on existential depth of meaning rather than adequate representation of an historical period which can be supplemented by other sources.

Finally, each volume also offers a preliminary interpretation of the relevance of the author and text for the present. The methodical interpretations seek to preserve the past historical meanings while also bringing them forward in a way that is relevant to life in a technologically developed and pluralistic secular culture. Each retrieval looks for those aspects that can open realistic possibilities for viable spiritual meaning in current lived experience. In the unfolding wisdom of the many volumes, many distinct aspects of the Christian history of spirituality converge into a fuller, deeper, more far-reaching, and resonant language that shows what in our time has been taken for granted, needs adjustment, or has been lost (or should be). The series begins with fifteen volumes but, like Cassian's *Conferences*, the list may grow.

About the Editors

ROGER HAIGHT is a Visiting Professor at Union Theological Seminary in New York. He has written several books in the area of fundamental theology. A graduate of the University of Chicago, he is a past president of the Catholic Theological Society of America.

ALFRED PACH III is an Associate Professor of Medical Sciences and Global Health at the Hackensack Meridian School of Medicine. He has a Ph.D. from the University of Wisconsin in Madison and an MDiv in Psychology and Religion from Union Theological Seminary.

AMANDA AVILA KAMINSKI is an Assistant Professor of Theology at Texas Lutheran University, where she also serves as Director of the program in Social Innovation and Social Entrepreneurship. She has written extensively in the area of Christian spirituality.

Past Light on Present Life:
Theology, Ethics, and Spirituality

Roger Haight, SJ, Alfred Pach III,
and Amanda Avila Kaminski, *series editors*

Available titles:

*Western Monastic Spirituality: John Cassian, Caesarius of Arles,
and Benedict*
On the Medieval Structure of Spirituality: Thomas Aquinas
Grace and Gratitude: Spirituality in Martin Luther
*Spirituality of Creation, Evolution, and Work: Catherine Keller
and Pierre Teilhard de Chardin*
*Spiritualities of Social Engagement: Walter Rauschenbusch
and Dorothy Day*
*Enlightened Spirituality: Immanuel Kant, Paul Tillich,
and Reinhold Niebuhr*
*Retrieving the Spiritual Teaching of Jesus: Sandra Schneiders,
William Spohn, and Lisa Sowle Cahill*
*From the Monastery to the City: Hildegard of Bingen
and Francis of Assisi*
A Civic Spirituality of Sanctification: John Calvin
*Finding God in a World Come of Age: Karl Rahner
and Johann Baptist Metz*

Printed in the USA
CPSIA information can be obtained
at www.ICGtesting.com
JSHW081202300824
69030JS00002B/11